The Illustrated

Jesus

Through the Centuries

JAROSLAV PELIKAN

THE ILLUSTRATED

Jesus

THROUGH THE

CENTURIES

YALE UNIVERSITY PRESS   New Haven & London

Published with assistance from

the Charles A. Coffin Fund.

The illustrations for this book were selected by Judy Metro,

with assistance from Larisa Heimert.

Designed by Richard Hendel

Production Controller: Mary Mayer

Set in Minion type by Highwood Typographic Services,

Hamden, Connecticut

Printed in Italy by Conti Tipocolor

Library of Congress Cataloging-in-Publication Data

Pelikan, Jaroslav Jan, 1923–
    The illustrated Jesus through the centuries / Jaroslav Pelikan.
        p.   cm.
    Rev. ed. of: Jesus through the centuries. c1985.
    Includes index.
    ISBN 0-300-07268-6 (cl : alk. paper)
    1. Jesus Christ—History of doctrines. 2. Jesus Christ—
Influence. I. Pelikan, Jaroslav Jan, 1923–   Jesus through the
centuries. II. Title.
BT198.P44 1997
232.9'04—dc21   97-7360
                                               CIP

A catalogue record for this book is available from the British Library.

10 9 8 7 6 5 4 3 2 1

To the Benedictines of Saint John's Abbey

Collegeville, Minnesota

nihil amori Christi praeponere

CONTENTS

I think I have always wanted to write this book. Having described, in *The Christian Tradition,* the history of the significance of the person and work of Jesus Christ for the faith and teaching of the Christian church, I am turning here to the other half of the story: his place in the general history of culture.

Clemenceau once remarked that war was entirely too important a matter to be left to the military. So also, Jesus is far too important a figure to be left only to the theologians and the church. And the invitation to deliver the William Clyde DeVane Lectures at Yale, public lectures in an academic setting, gave me just the opportunity I needed to write the book I had always wanted to write. The audiences at the lectures represented both town and gown—all ages, social backgrounds, educational levels, and religious persuasions. That is as well the kind of audience for whom the book is intended. Therefore I have sought, in citing my sources, to make use, if at all possible, of generally available editions, adopting and adapting earlier translations (including my own) without a pedantic explanation each time; biblical quotations are usually from the Revised Standard Version.

I have been greatly aided by listeners and students, colleagues and critics, to all of whom I am pleased to express my thanks. Special thanks are due my editors, John G. Ryden and Barbara Hofmaier, for bringing a sensitive ear and an impeccable taste to the improvement of my manuscript and for saving me from inelegancies and howlers.

The dedication is the expression of my fraternal devotion to my *fratres* at the Abbey of Saint John the Baptist in Collegeville, Minnesota, of whose Benedictine family I am proud to be an adopted son.

The gracious response of readers to *Jesus Through the Centuries* in its original edition, which has attained a circulation of more than 100,000 copies, as well as in the translations that have appeared in more than a dozen languages so far, has encouraged the publisher, and then the author, to contemplate the possibility of preparing an illustrated edition, with many times the number of pictures and a corresponding reduction of text.

This does not, then, replace the text edition, to which readers of this volume are encouraged to continue to turn for the identification and documentation of quotations in footnotes, for further readings, and for more complete exposition. But if the proved holds that "a picture is worth a thousand words" (or even "more than ten thousand words," in the Chinese version of the proverb as given by Bartlett), then the net content of the book has been greatly expanded. In this edition, too, I have adhered to the practice of usually quoting the Revised Standard Version of the Bible, but in a few places I have found some other English translation to be preferable, without pedantically calling attention to the differences.

The difficult and delicate task of suggesting these changes was first undertaken by Otto Bohlmann of the Editorial Department of Yale University Press, whose careful reading and pruning encouraged me to review each chapter thoroughly. Judy Metro made literally hundreds of suggestions of possible illustrations, and Laura Jones Dooley reviewed the text with her customary thoroughness and skill.

Strong Son of God, immortal Love,
Whom we, that have not seen thy face,
By faith, and faith alone, embrace,
Believing where we cannot prove. . . .
Our little systems have their day;
They have their day and cease to be:
They are but broken lights of thee,
And thou, O Lord, art more than they.
—*Alfred Lord Tennyson,* In Memoriam

Introduction

Regardless of what anyone may personally think or believe about him, Jesus of Nazareth has been the dominant figure in the history of Western culture for almost twenty centuries. If it were possible, with some sort of supermagnet, to pull up out of that history every scrap of metal bearing at least a trace of his name, how much would be left? It is from his birth that most of the human race dates its calendars, by his name that millions curse, and in his name that millions pray.

"Jesus Christ is the same yesterday and today and for ever. Do not be led away by diverse and strange teachings" (Heb. 13:8–9). With these words the New Testament admonished its readers to remain loyal to the deposit of the authentic and authoritative tradition of Christ, as this had come down to them

To understand why the figure of Jesus holds such endless fascination for modern men and women but also why they find it so difficult simply to go on repeating what previous ages of faith said about him, few works of literature are as instructive or as moving as In Memoriam *by Alfred Lord Tennyson, poet laureate to Queen Victoria. Tennyson strove, by "believing where we cannot prove," to be loyal in his own way to Jesus as "Strong Son of God, immortal Love." His faith was shaken and his doubt reinforced when his beloved friend and prospective brother-in-law, Arthur Henry Hallam, died in 1833.*

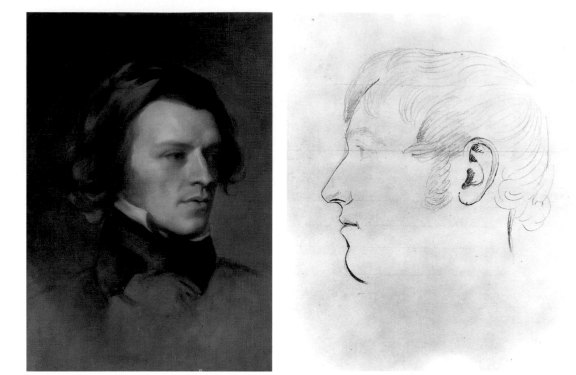

through the apostles of the first Christian generation, some of whom were still living. "The same yesterday and today and for ever" eventually came to have the metaphysical and theological significance that Jesus Christ was, in his eternal being, "the image of the unchangeable God, and therefore likewise unchangeable." But for the purposes of this book, it is the historical import of this phrase that must chiefly engage our attention. For, as will become evident in considerable detail before this history of images of Jesus through the centuries is finished, it is not sameness but kaleidoscopic variety that is its most conspicuous feature. "Each successive epoch," Albert Schweitzer once said, "found its own thoughts in Jesus, which was, indeed, the only way in which it could make him live"; for, typically, one "created him in accordance with one's own character."

This book explores, in word and image, what it was that each epoch found in Jesus and brought to its portrayal of him. For each age, the life and teachings of Jesus represented an answer (or, more often, *the* answer) to the most fundamental questions of human existence and human destiny, and it was to the figure of Jesus as set forth in the Gospels that those questions were addressed. If we want to comprehend the answers these previous centuries found there, we must penetrate to their questions, which in most instances will not be our own questions and in many instances may not even be explicitly their own questions. During the past two thousand years, few issues if any have so persistently brought out the fundamental assumptions of each epoch as has the attempt to

Roadside crosses in Anglo-Saxon Northumbria not only served as constant reminders of the death and resurrection of Jesus; but on one of them, the Ruthwell Cross, the reminder took the form of the Old English poem about Christ the young hero, The Dream of the Rood, *inscribed in letters of the runic alphabet.*

Intended for devotional use by travelers of the noble and royal classes, in this case Queen Isabella of Castile, Books of Hours often contained, in addition to prayers and biblical texts for meditation, miniature paintings, many of them quite exquisite, of biblical personages and events, including here the crucifixion of Christ and the deposition of his body from the cross.

come to terms with the meaning of the figure of Jesus of Nazareth. Conversely, the history of the images of Jesus illustrates simultaneously the continuities and the discontinuities of the past two millennia. One consequence of the discontinuity is the great variety and unevenness in the concepts and terms that have been used to describe him, from the most naive and unsophisticated to the most profound and complex. Whatever blurring of his image the welter of portraits of Jesus may create for the eyes of a faith that wants to affirm him as "the same yesterday and today and for ever," that very variety is a treasure trove for the history of culture. Nor is the portrait of Jesus in any epoch confined to the history of faith, central though it is for that history. For, in the words of the Gospel of John, "from his fulness [*plērōma*] have we all received, grace upon grace" (John 1:16)—a fullness that has proved to be inexhaustible as well as irreducible to formulas, whether dogmatic or antidogmatic; for, in Tennyson's words, "our little systems have their day," but he is always "more than they."

This is, then, neither a life of Jesus nor a history of Christianity as a movement or an institution. The invention of a genre of biographical literature known as the *Life of Jesus* is, strictly speaking, a phenomenon of the modern period, when scholars came to believe that by applying the methodology of a critical historiography to the source materials in the Gospels they would be able to reconstruct the story of his life. Naturally, the reconstructions of the life of Jesus in any period, beginning with the Gospels, will serve as indispensable artifacts of this history of Jesus through the centuries. But we shall be concerned here with more than the history of ideas, theological or nontheological or antitheological. In this new and illustrated format of the book, the efforts to portray the person of Jesus in visual form are central to the story. This they will be not only when, as in the Byzantine empire of the eighth and ninth centuries and again in the Reformation of the sixteenth century, the legitimacy of such depictions became a subject of intense discussion, with far-reaching implications for the history of art and aesthetics as well as for the history of politics. The portrayals of Christ in such works of art as roadside crosses in Anglo-Saxon Northumbria or Carolingian miniatures or Renaissance paintings will also provide us with the raw material for a cultural history of Jesus. Similarly, throughout we shall be drawing upon works of literature, from the Old English *Dream of the Rood* through Dante's *Divine Comedy* to Dostoyevsky's *Brothers Karamazov*, in order to assess the impact of Jesus on culture.

The most inclusive conceptual framework for this range of images is provided by the Platonic triad of the Beautiful, the True, and the Good, which itself has played a significant role in the history of Christian thought. Corresponding in some respects to that classical triad, though by no means identical with it, is the biblical triad of Jesus Christ as the Way, the Truth, and the Life (John 14:6), "the true light that enlightens every man" (John 1:9).

In a set of public lectures delivered at the University of Berlin in the academic year

1899–1900, that university's most renowned scholar, Adolf von Harnack, undertook to answer the question "What is Christianity?" The book that came out of his lectures opens with words that can well form the conclusion of this introduction as well: "The great English philosopher, John Stuart Mill, once commented that 'mankind can hardly be too often reminded that there was once a man named Socrates.' That is correct; but it is even more important to remind mankind that a man named Jesus Christ once stood in their midst." The words and images in this book represent a series of such reminders "through the centuries."

Come, O come, Immanuel,
And ransom captive Israel.
—Veni, Veni, Immanuel
  medieval antiphon

1 ✣ The Rabbi

The study of the place of Jesus in the history of human culture must begin with the New Testament, on which all subsequent representations have been based. But the presentation of Jesus in the New Testament is itself a representation, resembling a set of paintings more than a photograph.

In the decades between the time of the ministry of Jesus and the composition of the various Gospels the memory of what Jesus had said and done circulated in the form of an oral tradition. The apostle Paul, writing to the congregation at Corinth in about A.D. 55 (twenty years or so after the life of Jesus), reminded them that during his visit a few years before, probably in the early fifties, he had orally "delivered to you as of first importance what I also received" still earlier, thus perhaps in the forties, concerning the death and res-

As far as we know, the first event in the life of Jesus to be written down was his institution of the Lord's Supper (1 Cor. 11:23–26), within the setting of the Jewish Passover. As an observant Jew, Jesus would have celebrated the Passover annually all his life, first with his own family of Mary and Joseph, then with the family of his disciples. Dante Gabriel Rossetti provided a commentary on his painting of the Passover in a sonnet: "What shadow of Death the Boy's fair brow subdues / Who holds that blood wherewith the porch is stained / . . . And Mary culls the bitter herbs ordained."

urrection of Jesus (1 Cor. 15:1–7) and the institution of the Lord's Supper (1 Cor. 11:23–26). Chronologically and even logically, therefore, there was a tradition of the church before there was a New Testament, or any book of the New Testament. By the time the materials of the oral tradition found their way into written form, they had passed through the life and experience of the church, which laid claim to the presence of the Holy Spirit of God. It was to the action of that Spirit that Christians would attribute the composition of the

books of the "New Testament," as they began to call it, and before that of the "Old Testament," as they began to describe the Hebrew Bible.

It is obvious—and yet, to judge by the tragedies of later history, not at all obvious—that Jesus was a Jew, so that the first attempts to understand his message took place within the context of Judaism. The New Testament was written in Greek, but the language Jesus and his disciples usually spoke seems to have been Aramaic, a Semitic tongue related to Hebrew but not identical with it. Aramaic words and phrases are scattered throughout the Gospels and other early Christian books, reflecting the language in which various sayings and liturgical formulas had been repeated before the transition to Greek became complete. These include such familiar words as *Hosanna,* as well as the cry of dereliction of Jesus on the cross, *Eloi, Eloi, lama sabachthani?* (Mark 15:34)—"My God, my God, why hast thou forsaken me?" (which in the Hebrew of Psalm 22 was *Eli, Eli, lama azavtani?*). Alongside *Immanuel,* "God with us"—the Hebrew title given to the child in the prophecy of Isaiah (7:14) and applied by Matthew (1:23) to Jesus, but not used to address him except in such apostrophes as the medieval antiphon *Veni, Veni, Immanuel* that forms the epi-

The Gospels give us only one glimpse to satisfy—or to pique—our curiosity about the childhood of Jesus. In Holman Hunt's Finding of the Saviour in the Temple, *the incident narrated in Luke 2:41–52 epitomizes the ambivalence of his relation to the Jewish tradition. His parents find him seated among the teachers of the Mosaic law and confounding them with his questions and answers; but he gently rebukes the reproof of his parents by asking, "Did you not know that I must be in my Father's house?"—referring to the Jewish temple in the Holy City of Jerusalem.*

Although the buildings at the left are probably Muslim rather than Jewish, the use of Near Eastern architecture in the fifteenth-century Avignon Pietà *may be taken, together with for example the dramatic upsurge in the study of Hebrew, as part of the growing interest of the later Middle Ages and Renaissance in relating the historical figure of Jesus to his roots in Israel.*

graph to this chapter—four Aramaic words appear as titles for Jesus: *Rabbi,* or teacher; *Amēn,* or prophet; *Messias,* or Christ; and *Mar,* or Lord.

The most neutral and least controversial of these words is probably *Rabbi,* along with the related *Rabbouni.* Except for two passages, the Gospels apply the Aramaic word only to Jesus; and if we conclude that the title "teacher" or "master" (*didaskalos* in Greek) was intended as a translation of that Aramaic name, it seems safe to say that it was as Rabbi that Jesus was known and addressed. Yet the Gospels seem to accentuate the differences, rather than the similarities, between Jesus and the other rabbis. As the scholarly study of the Judaism of his time has progressed, however, both the similarities and the differences have become clearer.

Luke tells us (4:16–30) that after his baptism and temptation by the devil, he "came to Nazareth, where he had been brought up; and he went to the synagogue, as his custom was, on the sabbath day. And he stood up to read." Following the customary rabbinical pattern, he took up a scroll of the Hebrew Bible, read it, presumably provided an Aramaic

translation-paraphrase of the text, and then commented on it. The words he read were from Isaiah 61:1–2: "The Spirit of the Lord is upon me, because he has anointed me to preach good news to the poor. He has sent me to proclaim release to the captives and re-covering of sight to the blind, to set at liberty those who are oppressed, to proclaim the acceptable year of the Lord." But instead of doing what a rabbi would normally do, apply the text to the hearers by comparing and contrasting earlier interpretations, he declared: "Today this scripture has been fulfilled in your hearing." Although the initial reaction to this audacious declaration was said to be wonderment "at the gracious words which pro-ceeded out of his mouth," his further explanation produced the opposite reaction, and everyone was "filled with wrath."

Behind the confrontations between Jesus as Rabbi and the representatives of the rab-binical tradition, the affinities are nevertheless clearly discernible in the forms in which his teachings appear in the Gospels. One of the most familiar is the question and answer, with the question often phrased as a teaser. A woman had seven husbands (in series, not in parallel): whose wife will she be in the life to come (Matt. 22:23–33)? Is it lawful for a devout Jew to pay taxes to the Roman authorities (Matt. 22:15–22)? What must I do to in-herit eternal life (Mark 10:17–22)? Who is the greatest in the kingdom of heaven (Matt. 18:1–6)? The one who puts the question acts as a straight man, setting up the opportunity for Rabbi Jesus to drive home the point, often by standing the question on its head.

As Jesus' parable of the prodigal son (Luke 15:11–32) is visualized by James Tissot, the emphasis falls on the prodigal's contrition and the father's forgiveness. Yet the parable applies not only to individuals but to "the return of the prodigal" Gentiles accomplished by Christ. By that reading, the elder brother stands for the people of Israel, to whom the father says, "Son, you are always with me, and all that is mine is yours," which means that the covenant of God with Israel is eternal.

The repeated statements in the Gospels that the common people heard Jesus gladly and that he spoke with authority have inspired painters as well as other interpreters of the longest consecutive account of his public preaching, the Sermon on the Mount (Matt. 5–7), to show Jesus the Rabbi and Teacher in the light of how his discourse was received by his hearers, including those who obviously belonged to the peasant class.

To the writers of the New Testament, however, the most typical form of the teachings of Jesus was the parable: "He said nothing to them without a parable" (Matt. 13:34). But the Greek word *parabolē* was taken from the Septuagint, the Jewish translation of their Bible into Greek. Thus here, too, the evangelists' accounts of Jesus as a teller of parables make sense only in the setting of his Jewish background. Interpreting his parables on the basis of that setting alters conventional explanations of his comparisons between the kingdom of God and incidents from human life. Thus the point of the parable of the prodigal son (Luke 15:11–32), better called the parable of the elder brother, is in the closing words of the father to the elder brother, who stands for the people of Israel: "Son, you are always with me, and all that is mine is yours. It was fitting to make merry and be glad, for this your brother was dead, and is alive; he was lost, and is found." The historic covenant between God and Israel was permanent, and it was into this covenant that other peoples, too, were now being introduced.

The oscillation between describing the role of Jesus as Rabbi and attributing to him a new and unique authority made additional titles necessary. One such was *Prophet,* as in the acclamation on Palm Sunday (Matt. 21:11), "This is the prophet Jesus from Nazareth of Galilee." Probably the most intriguing version of it is once again in Aramaic (Rev. 3:14): "The words of the Amen, the faithful and true witness." The word *Amen* was the formula of affirmation to end a prayer, as in the farewell charge of Moses to the people of Israel, where each verse concludes (Deut. 27:14–26): "And all the people shall say, 'Amen.'" In the

Part of Paul's argument to the Romans that they, as Gentiles, had been "grafted" on to the olive tree of Israel (Rom. 11:17) was his use of the dramatic event that was to be memorialized in The Sacrifice of Isaac *by Lovis Corinth, after Rembrandt, as a typological anticipation of salvation in Christ. Like Father Abraham, who in obedience to God's mysterious command had been willing to offer up Isaac his son (Gen. 2:1–14), God "did not spare his own Son but gave him up for us all" (Rom. 8:32).*

It is well-nigh impossible to follow the Gospel narratives of the life of Jesus without some acquaintance with the geography of Palestine, and especially of Jerusalem, shown as it looks today. The photograph discloses another reason for the historic importance of Jerusalem. The three monotheisms of the Book—Judaism as represented by the Wall, Christianity as expressed in the onion domes of the Russian Orthodox church, and Islam as enshrined in the Dome of the Rock—all call it the Holy City, which is what it was also for Jesus.

New Testament an extension of the meaning of *Amen* becomes evident in the Sermon on the Mount: *Amēn legō hymin,* "Truly, I say to you." Some seventy-five times throughout the four Gospels *Amen* introduces an authoritative pronouncement by Jesus. As the one who had the authority to make such pronouncements, Jesus was the Prophet. The word *prophet* here means chiefly not one who *foretells,* although the sayings of Jesus do contain many predictions, but one who is authorized to speak on behalf of Another and to *tell forth.* In the Sermon on the Mount, Jesus is quoted as asserting (Matt. 5:17–18): "Think not that I have come to abolish the law and the prophets; I have come not to abolish them but to fulfil them. For truly [*amēn*], I say to you, till heaven and earth pass away, not an iota, not a dot, will pass from the law until all is accomplished." That affirmation of the permanent validity of the law of Moses is followed by a series of specific quotations from the law, each introduced with the formula "You have heard that it was said to the men of old"; each such quotation is then followed by a commentary opening with the magisterial formula "*But I say to you*" (Matt. 5:21–48). The commentary is an intensification of the commandment, to include not only its outward observance but the inward spirit and motivation of the heart. All these commentaries are an elaboration of the warning that the righteousness of the followers of Jesus must exceed that of those who followed other doctors of the law (Matt. 5:20).

The conclusion of the Sermon on the Mount confirms the special status of Jesus as not only Rabbi but Prophet (Matt. 7:28–8:1): "And when Jesus finished these sayings, the crowds were astonished at his teaching, for he taught them as one who had authority, and not as their scribes. When he came down from the mountain, great crowds followed him." Then there come several miracle stories. The New Testament does not attribute the power of performing miracles only to Jesus and his followers (Matt. 12:27), but it does cite the miracles as substantiation of his standing as Rabbi-Prophet. That identification of Jesus was a means both of affirming his continuity with the prophets of Israel and of asserting his superiority to them as *the* Prophet whose coming they had predicted and to whose authority they had been prepared to yield. In Deut. 18:15–22, God tells Moses, and through him the people, that he "will raise up for them a prophet like me from among you," to whom the people are to pay heed. In its biblical context, this is the authorization of Joshua as the legitimate successor of Moses, but in the New Testament and in later Christian writers, the prophet to come is taken to be Jesus-Joshua. He is portrayed as the one Prophet in whom the teaching of Moses was fulfilled and yet superseded, the one Rabbi who both satisfied the law of Moses and transcended it; for "the law was given through Moses; grace and truth came through Jesus Christ" (John 1:17). To describe such a revelation of grace and truth, the categories of Rabbi and Prophet were necessary but not sufficient. Therefore later anti-Muslim Christian apologists would find Islam's identification of Jesus as a great prophet and forerunner to Muhammad to be inadequate and

"I am a servant of God. He has given me a Book and made me a prophet," Jesus says in the Qur'ān at sura 19:30, "Maryam," devoted to the Virgin Mary. Beginning already with the first anti-Muslim apologists, Christians have repeatedly been surprised by the exalted language in which the Qur'ān describes Jesus and his mother. Denied conventional religious art by Allah's prohibition of images, Muslim artists lavished their aesthetic creativity on the calligraphy of the Qur'ān.

hence inaccurate, so that the potential of the figure of Jesus the Prophet as a meeting ground between Christians and Muslims has never been fully realized.

For Rabbi and Prophet yielded to two other categories, each of them likewise expressed in an Aramaic word and then in its Greek translation: *Messias,* the Aramaic form of "Messiah," translated into Greek as *ho Christos,* "Christ," the Anointed One (John 1:41, 4:25); and *Marana,* "our Lord," in the liturgical formula *Maranatha,* "Our Lord, come!" translated into Greek as *ho Kyrios* (1 Cor. 16:22). The future belonged to these titles and to the identification of him as the Son of God and second person of the Trinity. But in the process of establishing themselves, *Christ* and *Lord,* as well as even *Rabbi* and *Prophet,* often lost much of their Semitic content. To the Christian disciples of the first century the conception of Jesus as Rabbi was self-evident, to the Christian disciples of the second century it was embarrassing, to the Christian disciples of the third century and beyond it was obscure.

The beginnings of this de-Judaization of Christianity are visible already within the New Testament. With Paul's decision to "turn to the Gentiles" (Acts 13:46) after having begun his preaching in the synagogues, and then with the destruction of the temple in A.D. 70, the Christian movement increasingly became Gentile rather than Jewish in its constituency and outlook. In that setting the Jewish elements of the life of Jesus had to be explained to Gentile readers (for example, John 2:6). The Acts of the Apostles can be read as a tale of two cities: its first chapter, with Jesus and his disciples after the resurrection, is set in Jerusalem; but its last chapter reaches its climax with the final voyage of the apostle Paul, in the simple but pulse-quickening sentence "And so we came to Rome."

Recently, scholars have not only put the picture of Jesus back into the setting of first-century Judaism; they have also rediscovered the Jewishness of the New Testament, and particularly of Paul. His epistle to the Romans (9–11) is the description of his struggle over the relation between church and synagogue, concluding with the prediction and the promise: "And so all Israel will be saved"—not, it should be noted, converted to Christianity, but *saved,* because, in Paul's words, "as regards election they are beloved for the sake of their forefathers. For the gifts and the call of God are irrevocable" (Rom. 11:26–29). This reading of the mind of Paul in Romans gives special significance to his many references to the name of Jesus Christ there: from "descended from David according to the flesh . . . Jesus Christ our Lord" in the first chapter, to "the preaching of Jesus Christ," which "is now disclosed and through the prophetic writings is made known to all nations" in the final sentence. Here Jesus Christ is, as Paul says of himself elsewhere, "of the people of Israel . . . , a Hebrew born of Hebrews" (Phil. 3:5). The very issue of universality, supposedly the distinction between Paul and Judaism, was, for Paul, what made it necessary that Jesus be a Jew. For only through the Jewishness of Jesus could the covenant of God with Israel, the gracious gifts of God, and his irrevocable calling become available to

To visualize the declaration of the apostle Paul that "Jesus Christ our Lord" was "descended from David according to the flesh" (Rom. 1:3), combined with the prophecy that "there shall come forth a shoot from the stump of Jesse, and a branch shall grow out of his roots" (Isa. 11:1), many medieval biblical manuscripts and stained glass windows traced his genealogy in the form of a Tree of Jesse, from the father of David until the Virgin Mary and her Son.

all people in the whole world, also to the Gentiles, who "were grafted in their place to share the richness of the olive tree"—namely, the people of Israel (Rom. 11:17).

No one can consider the topic of Jesus as Rabbi and ignore the subsequent history of the relation between the people to whom Jesus belonged and the people who belong to Jesus. That relation runs like a red line through much of the history of culture, and after the events of the twentieth century we have a unique responsibility to be aware of it as we study the history of the images of Jesus through the centuries. The question is easier to ask than it is to answer, and it is easier to avoid than it is to ask at all. But ask it we must: Would there have been such anti-Semitism, would there have been so many pogroms, would there have been an Auschwitz, if every Christian church and every Christian home had focused its devotion on images of Mary not only as Mother of God and Queen of Heaven but also as the Jewish maiden and the New Miriam, and on icons of Christ not only as the Cosmic Christ but also as Rabbi Jesus of Nazareth, the Son of David, come to ransom a captive Israel and a captive humanity?

Jesus the Rabbi lived as a Jew, and he died as a Jew. Even while he was dying on the cross (Mark 15:34), he recited words from the Jewish Scriptures (Ps. 22:1). To a degree that is rare among depictions of the crucifixion, Marc Chagall's Yellow Crucifixion *of 1943, painted in a world that was about to know the horror of Auschwitz, emphasizes the Jewishness of Jesus in life and in death. Jesus wears the phylacteries of a devout Jew on his head, he has prayer straps on his arm, and at his right hand is the scroll of the Torah.*

Crown him the Lord of years,
The Potentate of time,
Creator of the rolling spheres,
Ineffably sublime.
—Matthew Bridges and Godfrey Thring
   The Seraphs' Song

2 ✦ The Turning Point of History

The contemporaries of Jesus knew him as Rabbi, but this was a rabbi whose ministry of teaching and preaching had as its central content "the gospel of God: 'The time is fulfilled, and the kingdom of God is at hand; repent, and believe in the gospel'" (Mark 1:14–15). Many of his early followers found it unavoidable to describe him as Prophet, but further reflection led them to specify what was distinctive about his prophetic mission: "In many and various ways God spoke of old to our fathers by the prophets; but in these last days he has spoken to us by a Son, whom he appointed the heir of all things, through whom also he created the world. He reflects the glory of God and bears the very stamp of his nature, upholding the universe by his word of power" (Heb. 1:1–3).

Jesus, standing "in the midst of the lampstands" (Rev. 1:12, 17), was identified as "the first and the last"—that is, the Lord of history and the Turning Point of History— when, in the last book of the New Testament (Rev. 11:15), "the seventh angel blew his trumpet, and there were loud voices in heaven, saying, 'The kingdom of the world has become the kingdom of our Lord and of his Christ, and he shall reign for ever and ever'"—a verse that resounds in the "Hallelujah Chorus" of George Frideric Handel's Messiah.

It is obvious from these and other statements of the early generations of Christian believers that as they carried out the task of finding a language that would not collapse under the weight of what they believed to be the significance of the coming of Jesus, they found it necessary to invent a grammar of time and history. It marked the crux of the issue between the church and the synagogue. Calling itself the new Israel and the true Israel, the church appropriated the schema of historical meaning that had arisen in the interpretation of the redemption of Israel accomplished by the exodus from Egypt, and adapted this schema to the redemption of humanity accomplished by the resurrection of Jesus Christ from the dead.

In language redolent of Ezekiel, Daniel, and later Jewish apocalypticism, one of his early followers heard Jesus call himself "the first and the last"—that is, the Lord of history (Rev. 1:17). The proclamation of Jesus himself about the kingdom of God, as well as such proclamations of his followers about him, resounded with contemporary accents of the fervid expectation that the victory of the God of Israel over the enemies of Israel, so long promised and so often delayed, was now at last to break. The Book of Acts describes the disciples of Jesus, even after the events of Good Friday and Easter, as inquiring of him just before he withdrew his visible presence from them, "Lord, will you at this time restore the kingdom to Israel?" to which Jesus replies, "It is not for you to know about times or seasons which the Father has fixed by his own authority" (Acts 1:6–7).

To leave it at that, however, would be too easy an evasion of the deepest problems. Repeatedly in Jesus' message the call for repentance and the summons to ethical change took as its ground the promise of the second coming: "This generation will not pass away till all these things take place. Heaven and earth will pass away, but my words will not pass away" (Matt. 24:34, Mark 13:30, Luke 21:32). But that generation did not live to see it all: the Son of Man did not come, and heaven and earth did not pass away. What did this disappointment of the apocalyptic hope of the second coming mean for the promise "My words will not pass away"? How did the person of Jesus retain its hold on an authority whose validity had apparently depended on the announcement of the impending end of history? Some scholars have sought to identify a crisis brought on by this disappointment as the major trauma of the early Christian centuries and the source for the rise of the institutional church and of the dogma about the person of Jesus. Somewhat surprisingly, this hypothesis finds little corroboration in the sources. What they disclose instead is the combination, side by side in the same minds, of an intense apocalyptic expectation that history will end and a willingness to live with the prospect of a continuance of human history—both of these finding expression in an increasing emphasis on the centrality of Jesus.

The North African thinker Tertullian, the first important Christian writer in Latin, well illustrates such a combination at the end of the second century. Warning believers against attending the degrading spectacles of Roman society, he urged Christians to wait

Repeatedly deposed and exiled for his loyalty to the confession of the Council of Nicaea in 325 that Jesus Christ, as the Son of God, was nothing less than "God from God, light from light, true God from true God, begotten not made, one in being [homoousios] with the Father," Athanasius, bishop of Alexandria in Egypt, also wrote a highly influential biography of the hermit Antony of Egypt as the imitator of Christ and thereby acquainted the West with Christian monasticism.

for the spectacle of the great day coming, when Christ would return in triumphal procession like a Roman conqueror. "We never march unarmed. . . . With prayer let us expect the angel's trumpet." And yet Tertullian could declare, in response to the charge of treason against the Roman empire, "We also pray for the emperors, for their ministers and for all in authority, for the welfare of the world, for the prevalence of peace, *for the delay of the final consummation.*" This prayer that the second coming be postponed represents nothing less than a new understanding of the meaning of history, an understanding according to which Jesus was not simply going to be the end of history by his second coming in the future but already was the Turning Point of History, a history that, even if it were to continue, had been transformed and overturned by his first coming in the past. As the hinge on which history turned, Jesus was the basis both for a new interpretation of the historical process and for a new historiography.

The new interpretation of the historical process began with the history of Israel, whose principal goal was now taken to be the life, death, and resurrection of Jesus. That made itself evident in the interpretation—and manipulation—of the prophetic tradition of the Jewish Scriptures. Describing the exodus of Israel from captivity, the prophet Hosea had said, speaking in God's name (Hos. 11:1), "When Israel was a child, I loved him, and out of Egypt I called my son"; but in the hands of the Christian evangelist, these words became a prediction of the flight to Egypt by the Holy Family to escape the murderous plot of King Herod (Matt. 2:15). The so-called enthronement psalms identified God as the true king of Israel, even when Israel had earthly kings like David, and Psalm 96:10 declared, "The Lord reigns"; but Christian apologists and poets inserted an explicit reference to the cross, so that it now became, "The Lord reigns *from the tree,*" words they then accused the Jews of having expunged. Christians ransacked the Hebrew Bible for references to Christ, compiling them in various collections and commentaries. The prophets of Israel had found their aim, and their end, in Jesus.

So it was as well with the kingdom of Israel, which Christians saw as having now become the authentic kingdom of God, over which the Crucified reigned "from the tree." For Augustine in the fifth century, King David, who had established Jerusalem as the capital of his kingdom, was "a son of the heavenly Jerusalem" even as king of that "earthly Jerusalem." He received the promise that "his descendants were to reign in Jerusalem in continual succession," and so he looked beyond himself and his kingdom to the kingship of Jesus Christ. A Christian review of the entire history of the divided kingdoms of Judah and Israel on the basis of what "the providence of God either ordered or permitted" showed that although the kings beginning with Rehoboam, the son of Solomon, did not "by their enigmatic words or actions prophesy what may pertain to Christ and the church," they did nevertheless point forward to Christ. For when the divided kingdoms were eventually reunited under one prince in Jerusalem, this was intended to anticipate Christ as the one and only King.

Responding to the charge that the coming of Christ and the adoption of Christianity had undermined the Roman empire and made it vulnerable to the incursions of the barbarians, Augustine of Hippo (d. 430) in The City of God, *elegantly decorated in its first printed edition, from Subiaco in 1467, made the case that Christ was indeed the Turning Point, without whose coming the course of human history did not make sense.*

The history of the changes and successive forms of the priesthood of Israel also made sense, according to the Christian argument, only when viewed from the perspective of Jesus as its Turning Point. The priesthood of Aaron and of "the sons of Levi" was temporary, and its substance had now at last appeared in the true high priest, Jesus Christ; for "he holds his priesthood permanently, because he continues for ever" (Heb. 7:24). Although in the New Testament the term *priest* does not ever refer explicitly to the ministers of the Christian church, nor even to the apostles of Jesus in their ministry, but only to Christ himself as priest or to the priests of the Old Testament or to all believers as priests, the church soon appropriated the term for its ordained clergy. The history of priesthood and sacrifice, therefore, was seen as having begun with the shadowy figure of Melchizedek, both king and priest, who by the Christian reading of Genesis, had sacrificed "bread and wine" (Gen. 14:18), and then as acquiring a definite form with Aaron. But it all led to Jesus Christ, from whom, in turn, it led to the priesthood of the church and the sacrifice of the Mass.

The first person to be called a "priest" in the Bible was "Melchizedek king of Salem," who "brought out [or in the Latin translation "offered," that is, sacrificed] bread and wine; he was priest of God Most High" (Gen. 14:18). Christ had "brought out bread and wine" in instituting the Eucharist, and by sacrificing himself he was supremely "priest of God Most High," thus both king and priest just as Melchizedek had been.

Thus the entire history of Israel had reached its turning point in Jesus as Prophet, Priest, and King. After the same manner, Jesus was identified as the turning point in the history of all the nations of the world, encapsulated in the history of the "mistress of nations," the Roman empire. The most massive and most influential monument of that identification was Augustine's *City of God.* "Not only before Christ had begun to teach, but even before he was born of the Virgin," Augustine contended, the history of Rome was

As the Lord of history and the Lord of heaven and earth, Jesus Christ was believed to have united heaven and earth, divine history and human history. A celestial map bears the title "The Heavens the Sphere of Christ," yet its circle encloses not only the stars but the historical figures of his saints and apostles, as well as Israel's crossing of the Red Sea.

characterized by the "grievous evils of those former times," which had become "intolerable and dreadful" not when Rome suffered military defeat but when it achieved military victory. "When Carthage was destroyed and the Roman republic was delivered from the great reason for its anxiety, then it was that a host of disastrous evils immediately resulted from the prosperous condition of things," above all the concentration of the "lust of rule" in the hands of the "more powerful few," while the "rest, worn and wearied," were subjected to its yoke. The expansion of the Roman empire, which accusers were blaming Christ for having reversed, was not an automatic benefit to the human race; for "if justice has been abolished, what is empire but a fancy name for larceny?"

And yet, the many undoubtedly great achievements of Rome could be traced, according to Augustine, to what the Roman political historian Sallust had identified in the first century B.C. as its ambition and its "desire for glory" and prestige, which restrained vice and immorality. In carrying out the purposes of history, the God who had acted and become known in Christ made use also of these qualities, which were the result not of luck or fortune or the power of the stars but of an "order of things and times, which is hidden from us, but thoroughly known to [God, who] . . . rules as lord and appoints as governor." Christ was, in the words of the epigraph to this chapter, "the Lord of years, the Potentate of time." This concept of an "order of things and times," what the Bible called a "series of generations," Augustine vigorously defended against the classical Greeek and Roman theory that history repeats itself, that "the same temporal event is reenacted by the same periodic revolutions" and cycles. Because "Christ died for our sins once and for all, and, rising from the dead, dies no more," it also had to be true that Plato had founded and taught in the Academy near Athens at only one point in history, not over and over again "during the countless cycles that are yet to be."

Time and history were, then, crucial for Augustine. But the events of Jesus' life, seen as the Turning Point of History, did not affect merely the interpretation of that history; they were responsible also for a revitalized and transformed interest in writing history. Augustine himself never put his hand to narrative history, but two Greek Christian authors from the fourth century, Eusebius of Caesarea and Athanasius of Alexandria, may serve as documentation for this new historiography, inspired by the person of Jesus Christ. Eusebius criticized his predecessors in Christian apologetics for concentrating on "arguments" rather than on "events." In his *Ecclesiastical History* he set out to rectify that imbalance by writing history in the light of the life of Jesus. The history of Jesus extended all the way to the beginnings of the human experience, for all those to whom God had appeared could be called Christians "in fact if not in name." It also extended forward into Eusebius's own time, for like the historians of classical antiquity, he concentrated on contemporary events. Yet according to Eusebius the decisive event in the history he was narrating had not been in his own lifetime but had taken place in the life of Jesus Christ.

The contemporary and sometime adversary of Eusebius, Athanasius, bishop of Alexandria, is remembered chiefly for his works of dogmatic and polemical theology. Yet in many ways his most influential book dealt with dogmatics and polemics only incidentally: *The Life of Antony,* a biography of the founder of Egyptian Christian monasticism. It stands as a prime example of the new historiography and new biography inspired by the life of Jesus in the Gospels, even though there are many affinities between it and earlier pagan biographies. Although the purpose of the book is to present Antony as the embod-

Although he was the author of the most powerful of all ancient and medieval books about the meaning of history, The City of God, *Augustine himself wrote no history as such. Instead, his thought inspired later Christian writers of history, such as the Venerable Bede (d. 735), who composed the* Life of Cuthbert *and the first history of England,* History of the English Church and People, *which was copied and decorated in a handsome edition only a few decades after his death.*

The tradition of biography was older than Christianity, but it received a new impetus through attention to the life of Jesus and therefore to the lives of his saints, as for example in the Venerable Bede's Life of Cuthbert *(opposite page). At the death of Cuthbert, "the departure of his holy soul to the Lord" was immediately communicated to Bede's monastic brothers at Lindisfarne and, eventually, through such artifacts as the twelfth-century illustrated manuscript of the* Life, *to later generations as well.*

iment of an ideal, that does not prevent Athanasius from depicting his life in concrete terms as an existential struggle. Throughout, it is an effort to describe Antony's life as "the work of the Savior in Antony." A medieval biography like the English historian Bede's *Life of Cuthbert* is an outstanding example of the tradition established by *The Life of Antony.* The life of Jesus in the Gospels was a turning point both for the life of Cuthbert (the life that he lived) and for *The Life of Cuthbert* (the life that Bede wrote).

Eventually the very calendar of Europe, which then became the calendar for most of the modern world, evolved into a recognition of the figure of Jesus as the Turning Point of History, the Turning Point both of history as process and of history as narrative. Chris-

The Christian affirmation
of the sovereignty of Christ over
both time and space transformed
calendars and maps, as Christians
began not only to count the years of
human history in relation to his
incarnation—years "before Christ"
(B.C.) and "years of our Lord"
(A.D.)—but to visualize the
continents and the nations on the
basis of their allegiance to him
rather than of their actual
geographical location. And so on
this medieval map the nations of
Western Christendom stand closer
to the Holy City of Jerusalem than
does Egypt!

tian historians from Luke to Eusebius and beyond retained the Roman system of dating events by the reigns of the emperors. The dates of the imperial reigns were in turn cited according to a chronology, computed from the legendary date of the founding of Rome by Romulus and Remus, as A.U.C., *Ab Urbe Condita*. The persecutions of the church under the emperor Diocletian led some Christians to date their calendars from the Age of the Martyrs. In a calendrical system still retained by the Christian Copts and by the Christians of Ethiopia, the fourth-century *Index to the Festal Letters of Athanasius* is arranged according to the Egyptian calendar of months and days within each year, but it identifies the year of the first *Festal Letter* as "the forty-fourth year of the Diocletian Era," that is, A.D. 327.

But in the sixth century a Scythian monk living in Rome, Dionysius Exiguus, proposed a new system of reckoning. It was to be named not for the pagan myth of the founding of Rome by Romulus and Remus, nor for the persecutor Diocletian, but for the incarnation of Jesus Christ, specifically for the day of the annunciation of his birth to the Virgin Mary by the angel Gabriel, 25 March, in the year 753 A.U.C. Dionysius Exiguus miscalculated by four to seven years, producing the anomaly by which Jesus was born in "4 B.C." Such trifles aside, Dionysius's identification of "the Christian era" gradually established itself, though the process required many centuries, and it is now universal. Henceforth the dates of history and biography are marked as A.D. and B.C., according to "the years of Our Lord." Biographies of his enemies have to be written this way, so that we speak of Nero as having died in A.D. 68 and of Stalin as having died in A.D. 1953. In this sense, and not only in this sense, everyone is compelled to acknowledge that because of Jesus of Nazareth history will never be the same.

Now the virgin is returning. . . .

A new human race is descending from the heights of heaven. . . .

The birth of a child, with whom the iron age of humanity will end and
    the golden age begin. . . .

Under your guidance, whatever vestiges remain of our ancient wickedness,

Once done away with, shall free the earth from its incessant fear. . . .

    For your sake, O child, the earth, without being tilled,

Will freely pour forth its gifts. . . .

Your very cradle shall pour forth for you

Caressing flowers. The serpent too shall die. . . .

Assume your great honors, for the time will soon be at hand,

Dear child of the gods, great offspring of Jove!

See how it totters—the world's vaulted might,

Earth, and wide ocean, and the depths of heaven,

All of them, look, caught up in joy at the age to come!

—*Vergil*, Fourth Eclogue

3 ✣ The Light of the Gentiles

"Nothing is so incredible," the American theologian Reinhold Niebuhr once observed, "as an answer to an unasked question." He went on to use that epigram as a basis to divide human cultures into those "where a Christ is expected" and those "where a Christ is not expected." But the followers of Jesus carried out their mission on the growing assumption that there was no culture "where a Christ is not expected" and that therefore, in his person and in his teaching, in his life and in his death, Jesus represented the divine fulfillment of an aspiration that was universal, what Ignatius of Antioch in the first century A.D. called "the ground for hoping that [all of humanity] may be converted and win their way to God," through Jesus the Christ, "our common name and our common hope."

In addressing the Gentile world, Christian thinkers sought to discover in Greco-Roman culture the questions to which the name of Jesus Christ was the answer; as had been prophesied of him in his infancy, he was "thy salvation, which thou hast prepared in the presence of all peoples, a light for revelation to the Gentiles, and for glory to thy people Israel" (Luke 2:30–32). By analogy with the techniques for interpreting the Hebrew Bible to portray Jesus as the glory of the people of Israel, there were several methods for interpreting him also as the light for revelation to the Gentiles: non-Jewish prophecies of a Christ; Gentile anticipations of the doctrine about Jesus; and pagan foreshadowings or "types" of the redemption achieved by his death.

Messianic hope and messianic prophecy were not the exclusive possession of Israel. "Even in other nations," Augustine said, "there were those to whom this mystery was revealed and who were also impelled to proclaim it." Job, Jethro the father-in-law of Moses, and Balaam the prophet were three such "Gentile saints," spoken of in the Hebrew Bible, with whose existence both the rabbis and the church fathers had to come to terms. Armed with such biblical warrant, Christian apologists found in Gentile literature other evidence of messianic prophecy that pointed forward to Jesus.

The most dramatic and most familiar was the prophecy of a "new order of the ages" by the Roman poet Vergil (who died in 19 B.C.) in the fourth of his *Eclogues,* from which the epigraph of this chapter derives. These words—which I have translated from Latin into as neutral, that is, nonbiblical, an English as possible—appeared to echo various biblical accents. They anticipated "a new heaven and a new earth" (Isa. 66:22); they looked forward to a new human race, whose citizenship would be of heaven, not of earth (Phil. 3:20); they predicted the abolition of the hereditary blight of wickedness that clung to human nature in this fallen world (Isa. 53:5); they even described the crushing of the serpent, as the consolation given to Adam and Eve in the Garden of Eden had promised (Gen. 3:15)—all of this brought about by the coming of the wondrous Virgin and by the birth of the divine Child (Isa. 7:14, 9:6). The *Fourth Eclogue* was claimed as a prophecy of Jesus by the emperor Constantine, in a Good Friday *Oration to the Saints* delivered perhaps in 313. Although Jerome was not prepared to accept the messianic interpretation of Vergil, Augustine agreed with Constantine that "it is of [Christ] that this most famous poet speaks." A setting of the Mass of Saint Paul, sung at Mantua until the end of the Middle Ages, contained the legend that the apostle had visited the grave of Vergil in Naples and had wept over not having come soon enough to find him alive. But the most unforgettable application of the *Fourth Eclogue* to the coming of Jesus is in Dante's *Purgatorio,* which quotes the verses of Vergil in Italian translation and then adds this salute to Vergil: "Through you I became a poet, through you a Christian."

The standing of the *Fourth Eclogue* as a prophecy about Jesus was enhanced by Vergil's reference to the authority of the Greco-Roman prophetess Cuma, the Cumaean Sibyl; Vergil spoke of her also in the *Aeneid* as singing "frightening riddles." There were several

As he probably still is today,
so in the Western Middle Ages the
favorite poet from classical antiquity
was Vergil. His standing was
enhanced by the belief that in his
Fourth Eclogue, *under the*
influence of the Old Testament
(Isa. 7:14, 9:6), he had prophesied
the birth of Christ from the Virgin.
Therefore Dante made Vergil the
guide through the nether regions
for Dante the pilgrim, as William
Blake's engraving shows the
Roman poet beckoning to
the Florentine poet.

collections of visions and sayings of the various sibylline oracles, one of the most important of which was destroyed by a fire in Rome's Capitol in 83 B.C. That provided an irresistible opportunity over the next several centuries for various groups—pagan, Jewish, and Christian—to tamper with the new collections of oracles, and entire books of Christian (or Christianized) sayings were interpolated into them. Christians quoted the sibylline oracles, albeit in a heavily doctored version, citing them as prophetic books with an authority derived from their inspiration by the Holy Spirit, which deserved to be equated with the authority of the Hebrew Bible itself. The sibyl was "at once prophetic and poetic." In the *Oration to the Saints,* Constantine also appealed to the sibyl, finding in her a poem whose first letters spelled the Greek words "Jesus Christ, Son of God, Savior, cross," which in turn were an acrostic for *ichthys,* the Greek word for fish, a symbol of

Christ—all of this predicted, so it was assumed, by a pagan Roman female prophet (though actually, of course, by some anonymous Christian forger).

The sibylline tradition was also especially useful as a source of verification for the coming of Christ to judgment at the end of the world. For already in their unalloyed pagan form, the sayings of the sibyl had apparently contained threats and warnings about a divine punishment to come. In Jewish and then especially in Christian hands, these threats became both more extensive and more explicit. Apologists for the Christian creed quoted the sibyl's prophecy that everything changeable and corruptible was going to be destroyed by God in the Last Judgment and quoted her as proof that God was the source of famines, plagues, and all other dire punishments. As a prophecy of the second coming of Christ to judge the quick and the dead, the oracles of the sibyl enjoyed wide favor in medieval theology and folklore, as well as art, especially the Italian art of the late Middle Ages and the Renaissance.

This Christianizing of the sibyl reached its artistic climax when, along the left and right walls of the Sistine Chapel, Michelangelo's ceiling frescoes depicted five sibyls and five Old Testament prophets in alternating figures. Both their size and their placement by Michelangelo can be taken to mean that he was in substantial agreement with the tradition in depicting the Delphic Sibyl and the prophet Isaiah as occupying jointly the position of witnesses who predicted the first and second comings of Christ. As such a prediction about Christ, the sayings of the sibyl were permanently enshrined in the words of the "Dies irae," sung at countless Requiem Masses:

> The day of wrath, that dreadful day
> Shall the whole world in ashes lay,
> As David and the Sibyl say.

A second method for portraying Jesus as the Light of the Gentiles was to find Gentile anticipations of Christian doctrines about him. The most complete formulation of this method comes from the Greek Christian theologian Clement of Alexandria. Though he was widely read in classical Greek literature, Clement consistently saw himself as a faithful pupil of Jesus, the divine Tutor, whom he described as "God in the form of man, stainless, the minister of his Father's will, the Word [Logos] who is God, who is in the Father, who is at the Father's right hand, and with the form of God is God." Yet the author of this or-

The parallelism between the Gentile and Hebrew prophets who had predicted the birth and the death of Jesus Christ was an essential part of Michelangelo's grand design for the Sistine Chapel, which encompassed the full range of human history, from the creation to the Last Judgment. Among the Gentile prophets of the coming of Christ, the Greco-Roman prophetess Cuma, the Cumaean Sibyl (opposite page, left), held pride of place, because it was she who had inspired Vergil, author of the Fourth Eclogue. *Among the Hebrew prophets the one with the most direct connection to Jesus was Isaiah (opposite page, right), who had prophesied of his birth from a virgin (Isa. 7:14), had announced that birth in the familiar words "To us a child is born" (Isa. 9:6), and had described the sufferings of Christ, who "was wounded for our transgressions" and "bruised for our iniquities" (Isa. 53:5).*

When, in the scene from book 12 of Homer's Odyssey, *here portrayed on a crater found at Vulci, Odysseus tells his companions to lash him to the mast so that they and he may vanquish the evil forces of the Sirens, he was, according to Clement of Alexandria, foreshadowing the cross to which Jesus, the Logos of God, was lashed, "who will be your pilot, and the Holy Spirit will bring you to anchor in the harbor of heaven," vanquishing the evil forces of the devil.*

Steeped as they were in the classical tradition, Greek-speaking Christians found it irresistible to make a connection between Jesus Christ, the divine Teacher, who lived and died in Jerusalem, and the greatest of all merely human teachers, Socrates, who lived and died in Athens. Both had brought a message that was divine in its origin and authority, and both were put to death by those who found that message threatening.

thodox confession was, at the same time and without any final sense of contradiction, an advocate of Platonic philosophy, to which he assigned a high and holy mission. "Perhaps," he was willing to suggest, "philosophy was given to the Greeks [by God] directly and primarily," although not permanently, but "until the Lord should call the Greeks." Paul had said (Gal. 3:24) that the law of Moses was a kind of tutor or "custodian until Christ came." In somewhat the same way, Clement maintained, philosophy was "a tutor to bring the Hellenic mind to Christ." "The real philosophy" as the Greeks had discovered it would lead to "the true theology" as Christ had disclosed it.

A third technique for identifying Jesus as the Light of the Gentiles no less than as the glory of the people of Israel was to look in classical history and literature for persons and events that could be interpreted as "types" and prefigurings of Jesus and of redemption through him. "A type," according to the definition of the Alexandrian theologian Origen (Clement's pupil), "is a figure that came before us in the [Old Testament] fathers, but is fulfilled in us." For example, when Joshua conquers Jericho, this deed of the first Joshua, son of Nun, foreshadows the redemption accomplished by the second Joshua, Jesus, son of Mary; for in Aramaic and in Greek the two names are the same. Thus "as Moses lifted

up the [bronze] serpent in the wilderness, so must the Son of man be lifted up [on the cross], that whoever believes in him may have eternal life" (John 3:14–15).

In his presentation of the arguments for Jesus to a rabbi named Trypho, the second-century apologist Justin Martyr maintained that wherever wood or a tree appeared in the Old Testament, this could be a type or figure of the cross. But when he turned to present the arguments for Jesus to a Roman emperor, Antoninus Pius, he drew upon non-Jewish sources and examples to set forth the case for the cross as "the greatest symbol of the power and rule" of Jesus. In the *Timaeus,* invoking what Iris Murdoch has called one of "the most memorable images in European philosophy," Plato had taught that in the creation of the universe the Demiurge had "split [the soul-stuff] into two halves and [made] the two cross one another at their centres in the form of the letter Chi." Repeating the standard claim of Jewish and Christian apologists that Plato had borrowed from the Hebrew Bible, Justin insisted that Plato, misunderstanding Moses "and not apprehending that it was the figure of the cross," had nevertheless said that the Logos, "the power next to the first God, was placed crosswise in the universe."

Among the examples in Justin's catalogue, one of the most intriguing is his symbol of the cross as a mast. At the very fountainhead of classical literature stood a "type" of the cross to correspond to the pole on which Moses had lifted up the bronze serpent, the story of Odysseus at the mast from the *Odyssey.* Odysseus addresses his companions: "You must tie me hard in hurtful bonds, to hold me fast in position upright against the mast." Clement of Alexandria made the most effective and profound use of this image as a foreshadowing of Jesus: "Tied to the wood [of the cross], you shall be freed from destruction. The Logos of God will be your pilot, and the Holy Spirit will bring you to anchor in the harbor of heaven." Various Byzantine commentaries on Homer carried out this image and in the process helped to protect the ancient classics against the misplaced zeal of religious bigotry.

In using the Hebrew Bible and the Jewish tradition to explain the meaning of Jesus, Christians had applied all three of these methods to their interpretation of Moses. When they addressed the message of Jesus to the Gentiles, Socrates performed a function similar to that of Moses. He was himself a type and forerunner of Christ. The divine Logos, who was to appear in Jesus, had been active in Socrates, denouncing the polytheism and devil-worship of the Greeks. As one who "lived reasonably, viz., in accordance with the Logos," Socrates was "a Christian before Christ," and like Christ he was put to death by the enemies of reason and the Logos. Socrates had likewise anticipated the Christian doctrine of life eternal. For even though the New Testament had asserted that Jesus "abolished death and brought life and immortality to light through the gospel" (2 Tim. 1:10), most early Christian thinkers did not take this to mean that there had not been any awareness of immortality before him. On the contrary, quoting the Book of Psalms together with Plato's

Jesus became, already in the second century, the fulfillment not only of Hebrew prophecy but of "philosophy which was given to the Greeks" in anticipation of Christ. Through medieval and modern times, the most popular adaptation of philosophy to Christian thought and of Christian thought to philosophy (translated into English by Chaucer and then by Queen Elizabeth I) was The Consolation of Philosophy, *Boethius's vision of Lady Philosophy, "the crown of whose head touched the heavens" (opposite page, right). For some reason, however, the work never mentions the name of Christ.*

Nowhere was the designation of Jesus Christ as the Light of the Gentiles and as the fulfillment of their needs and yearnings more strikingly dramatized than in the sermon of Paul on the Areopagus ("Mars Hill") in Athens. "What therefore you worship as unknown, this I proclaim to you," he declared (Acts 17:23). As Raphael's watercolor of 1516 shows them, various of the Athenians reacted with fascination, others with indifference.

Republic on the Final Judgment, Clement could conclude, "It follows from this that the soul is immortal," a doctrine on which Scripture and philosophy were agreed.

But Socrates and Plato could also serve as the source for prophecy even about the death of Jesus on the cross. In the course of listing various pagan prophecies about creation, the Sabbath, and other biblical themes, Clement came to one prophecy in the *Republic*, where, he said, "Plato all but predicts the history of salvation." Drawing a distinction between righteousness and unrighteousness, Glaucon, the interlocutor of Socrates, postulates that, instead of beings who are both righteous and unrighteous, as most of us are most of the time, there would arise one unrighteous man who is entirely unrighteous and one righteous man who is entirely righteous. Let this one righteous man now be accused of being in fact the worst of men. Let him, moreover, "remain steadfast to the hour of death, seeming to be unrighteous and yet being righteous." What will be the outcome? The answer must be (in the translation of Gilbert Murray) none other than this: "He shall be scourged, tortured, bound, his eyes burnt out, and at last, after suffering every evil, shall be impaled or crucified."

As Paul, the apostle of Jesus Christ, had said to the Greeks about "the Unknown God," so the successors of Paul went on to say to the Greeks and to all the Gentiles about "the Unknown Jesus": "What therefore you worship as unknown, this I proclaim to you" (Acts 17:23).

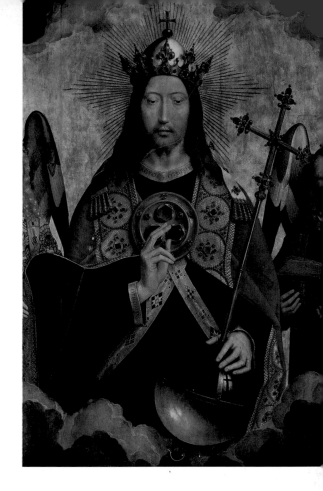

Thou hast conquered, O pale Galilean;

the world has grown gray from thy breath.

—*Algernon Charles Swinburne*, Hymn to Proserpine

4 ❖ The King of Kings

Even before Jesus was born, the Gospels inform us, the angel told his mother: "The Lord God will give to him the throne of his father David, and he will reign over the house of Jacob for ever; and of his kingdom there will be no end" (Luke 1:32–33). After his birth there came wise men from the East, asking (Matt. 2:2), "Where is he who has been born king of the Jews?" The entry into Jerusalem on Palm Sunday reminded his followers of the words of the prophet, "Behold, your king is coming to you, humble and mounted on an ass" (Matt. 21:5). The cross on which he died bore an inscription in three languages: "Jesus of Nazareth, the King of the Jews" (John 19:19). The last book of the New Testament, employing a title that had also been claimed by earthly monarchs, hailed him as "Lord of lords and King of kings" (Rev. 17:14).

And yet Pontius Pilate could ask him (John 18:37), "So you are a king?"

Pilate's question has been answered in many ways. For the title "King" did not remain on the cross; it moved out into the world of nations and of empires. And the cross itself moved out to decorate the crowns and flags and public buildings of empires and of nations—as well as the graves of those who died in their wars: as Augustine said, "That very cross on which he was derided, he has now imprinted on the brows of kings." The enthronement of Jesus as King of kings transformed the political life of a large part of the human race. As we shall see repeatedly in later chapters, much of the "divine right of kings" and of the theory of "holy war" rested on the presupposition that Jesus Christ was King, and so did much of the eventual rejection both of all war and of the divine right of kings. To trace the historical variations and permutations of the kingship of Jesus in its interaction with other political themes and symbols is to understand a large part of what is noble and a large part of what is demonic in the political history of the West: even the Nazi swastika, though older than Christianity in its form, was used as an obscene parody of the cross of Christ, as is evident from its very name in German, *Hakenkreuz*, "the hooked cross."

Sometimes accompanying the image of Jesus as King of kings was the expectation that he was about to establish his kingdom here on earth, in which the saints would rule with him for a thousand years. In substantiation of this millenarian hope for the coming kingdom, the writer of the Apocalypse heard voices in heaven shouting: "The kingdom of the world has become the kingdom of our Lord and of his Christ, and he shall reign for ever and ever" (Rev. 11:15). Yet this literal expectation of the reign of Christ was by no means universal among Christians even in the second century. The allegorical and the literal interpretations of the kingdom of Christ could both have answered Pilate's question by saying with Justin Martyr that "truly Christ is the everlasting King." Coming as it did

By its sheer size, Jacopo Tintoretto's enormous canvas of 1566–67, Christ Before Pilate *(opposite page), which is thirteen feet wide and eighteen feet high, makes it clear that Pilate's question, "So you are a king?" pitted the overt grandeur of Caesar and the Roman empire against the hidden grandeur of the Prisoner, over whom, as he said to Pilate, Rome and Pilate would "have no power unless it had been given you from above" (John 19:11), from the King of heaven—a claim that Pilate, and his emperor, Tiberius Caesar, could not even understand, much less acknowledge.*

"Be strong, and show yourself a man!" was the admonition Polycarp of Smyrna (above) heard through a voice from heaven before he was put to death for refusing to say "Caesar is Lord [Kyrios Kaisar]" and to offer incense to the emperor. "For eighty-six years I have been the servant [of Jesus Christ], and he never did me any injury," he replied. "How then can I blaspheme my King who saved me?"

According to Christian teaching, every legitimate ruler, even a pagan emperor, held office as a representative of the true God. The words of the New Testament, "There is no authority except from God, and those that exist have been instituted by God" (Rom. 13:1), were written under Nero, who persecuted Christians. Nevertheless, when the emperor Constantine became a Christian in the fourth century, that generalized divine sanction took on new meaning, as on this medal, where the emperor, larger than life, is receiving his crown directly from the hand of God.

from the representative of Tiberius Caesar, Pilate's question was to be echoed many times in the following centuries by the representatives of other Caesars. One of these asked the early Christian martyr Polycarp of Smyrna: "What harm is there in saying 'Caesar is Lord [*Kyrios Kaisar*],' and offering incense and saving your life?" Replied Polycarp, who was burned at the stake for his beliefs: "For eighty-six years I have been the servant [of Jesus Christ], and he never did me any injury. How then can I blaspheme my King who saved me?"

Alongside such pledges of allegiance to Jesus as the heavenly King over all earthly kings, however, there stand the repeated reassurances by apologists that this did not make the followers of Jesus disloyal to their earthly rulers. "When you hear that we are looking for a kingdom," they said to the emperor of Rome himself, "you suppose, without making any further inquiry, that we are speaking about a human kingdom." In fact, they insisted, they were not speaking about a political kingdom at all, but about a kingdom "that is with God." They cited as evidence of their loyalty the prayers "for the safety of our princes" that were being offered in Christian worship "to the eternal, the true, the living God, whose favor, beyond all others, they must themselves desire. . . . We pray for security to the

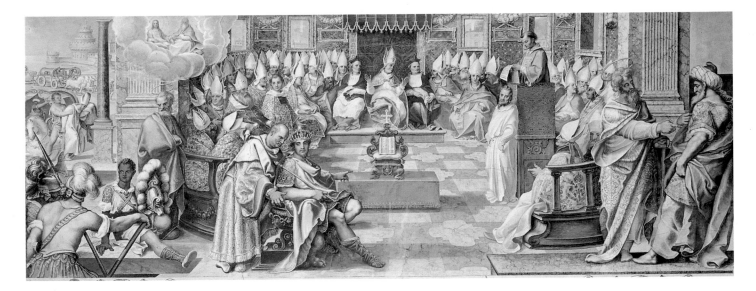

empire, for protection to the imperial house." What they refused to do was to treat the emperor as divine, to say "Kyrios Kaisar," and to swear by his "genius." The kingdoms of this present age had been established by God, not by the devil as some heretics maintained, and therefore were worthy of obedience under God, but obedience short of idolatry: "Render therefore to Caesar the things that are Caesar's, and to God the things that are God's" (Matt. 22:21). But as Jesus was King of all kings and Lord of all lords, not one in a series of lords, there was nothing due to Caesar that was not due also, and first, to God.

Christians did not look upon Jesus as the leader of a political revolution "from below" that would mean the end of the empire and its replacement by still another political system. And yet, despite the sincerity of their protestations that they prayed for the delay of the end of the world and for the health of the empire, they were all awaiting the second coming of Christ, which would "from above" bring the end of the world and therefore of the empire. The continuance of the Roman empire was the final obstacle to the end; for when Rome fell, the world would fall. One early Christian summarized this complex position with simple eloquence:

> Do you think that [Jesus] was sent [by God], as might be supposed, to establish some sort of political sovereignty [*tyrannis*], to inspire fear and terror? Not so. But in gentleness and meekness has He sent him, as a king would send a son who is himself a king. He sent him, as [God] sending God. . . . And He will send him [again] in judgment, and who shall endure his presence? . . . [Therefore] Christians are not distinguished from the rest of humanity either in locality or in speech or in customs. For they do not dwell off somewhere in cities of their own, neither do they use some different language, nor do they practice an extraordinary style of life. . . . But while they dwell in cities of Greeks and barbarians as the lot of each is cast, . . . the constitution of their citizenship is nevertheless quite amazing and admittedly paradoxical. They

Although Constantine was not baptized until just before his death and therefore could not participate fully in the sacramental life of the church, he did characterize himself as "bishop in externals" and was even called "equal to the apostles." Exercising those prerogatives, not only did he in 325 summon the first ecumenical council of the church at Nicaea, near Constantinople (seen in a fresco by Cesare Nebbia), but he intervened personally in its doctrinal deliberations.

Jesus was put to death under Roman law—whether legally or illegally is still debated. But ultimately he became a major force in the history of Roman law, through the legislation of Christian emperors beginning with Constantine I, then through the collection of this legislation in the Theodosian Code of 438, and eventually through the codification of the entire Roman law by Emperor Justinian in 529.

dwell in their own countries, but only as sojourners. . . . *Every foreign country is a fatherland to them, and every fatherland is a foreign country.*

That is one reason for the puzzling circumstance that some of the "best" emperors, the best morally as well as politically, like Marcus Aurelius and Diocletian—though also some of the worst, like Nero—also instituted some of the fiercest persecutions of Christians. Because Jesus was King, Christians could be provisionally loyal to Caesar; but because Jesus was King, they could not give Caesar the measure of loyalty that the best Caesars demanded for the Roman empire to be, as Vergil had said it would be, "the empire that will never end."

One eventuality they did not envisage was the possibility that Caesar himself might acknowledge Christ as King of kings. "The Caesars too would have believed in Christ," asserted the North African convert Tertullian, "if Christians could have been Caesars"; but that was a contradiction in terms. Yet that contradiction became a political reality early in the fourth century, when the emperor Constantine became a Christian, declaring his allegiance to Jesus Christ and adopting the cross as his official emblem before a decisive battle. At the hands of Eusebius, the first historian of the church and the biographer of Constantine, Constantine's conversion and military victory became a full-blown theology of history and an apologia for the idea of a Christian Roman empire. "The God of all, the Supreme Governor of the whole universe, by his own will appointed Constantine . . . to be prince and sovereign": this is how Eusebius begins his account. Constantine narrated to the historian under oath many years later that on 27 October 312, as he was praying, he "saw with his own eyes the trophy of a cross of light in the heavens above the sun, and bearing this inscription, 'Conquer by this!'" The entire army of Constantine, moreover, were also said to have witnessed the heavenly apparition and "were struck with amazement." After his victory Constantine ordered "a trophy of the Savior's passion, . . . the savior sign of the cross," to be placed in the hand of his own statue, which was to be erected in Rome, with the inscription: "By this savior sign, the true test of bravery, I saved and freed your city from the yoke of the tyrant, and restored the senate and the Roman people, freed, to their ancient fame and splendor." Rome had passed into the protection of Christ.

"As a thank offering to his Savior for the victories he had obtained over every foe," Constantine convoked the first ecumenical council of the church in 325 at Nicaea, named for *Nikē* (Victory), for the purpose of restoring concord to church and empire. The Council of Nicaea declared that Jesus as the Son of God was "begotten not created, one in being [*homoousios*] with the Father." That dogmatic formula was, according to Eusebius, the result of a direct personal intervention by Constantine himself (even though he had not yet been baptized, and would not be until just before his death in 337), when "our emperor, most beloved by God, began to reason concerning [Christ's] divine origin, and His

Praised by Gregory of Nazianzus as a "mighty Christ-loving city" and "the eye of the universe, in its exceeding strength by sea and land . . . the link between the Eastern and the Western shores, in which the extremities of the world from every side meet together," Constantinople or New Rome stood for eleven centuries (330–1453) in honor of Jesus as King of Kings, who ruled also over the realm of the Caesars.

existence before all ages: He was virtually in the Father without generation, even before He was actually begotten, the Father having always been the Father, just as [the Son] has always been a King and a Savior."

Once the Council of Nicaea had accepted these formulas, they became the law not only for the church but also for the empire. Only those who conformed to that "apostolic discipline," as the *Theodosian Code* of Roman law called it, would have the right to hold political office within the Christian empire. As a result of the events of the fourth century, it was necessary, for the next thousand years and more, to accept Christ as the eternal King if one wanted to be a temporal king. The effort of the emperor Julian (to whom Christians attached the epithet "the Apostate"), during his brief reign from 361 to 363, to reintroduce a reformed paganism ended with his death in battle. Hostile Christian legend described him as crying out as he fell, "At last thou hast conquered, O Galilean." That cry, enshrined in the lines of Algernon Charles Swinburne that form the epigraph to this chapter, may not have been historical, but the conquest by Christ the King was.

Nevertheless, that conquest did not of itself settle the question of political sover-

Early medieval Europe, including Rome itself, was theoretically a province of the "Roman" empire, governed from Constantinople through a deputy, or "exarch," in the Italian city of Ravenna. The arrival of the Germanic peoples made that theoretical authority even less enforceable than it already was, and the political future would belong to the German tribe that could ally itself with Old Rome in the person of the pope. On Christmas Day 800, the king of the Franks, Karl (known to us as Charlemagne), the central figure depicted among the statues from his burial shrine at Aachen, was crowned Roman emperor by the representative of Christ, Pope Leo III, also shown.

eignty, for it was possible to draw the lines of connection between the eternal kingship of the "pale Galilean" and the temporal kingship of earthly rulers in several different patterns. One theory was the one Constantine seems to have employed. His language to bishops and clergy was properly deferential, but behind the deference was the firm hand of one who knew where the real power lay. God the Father as King of the universe had conferred "all authority in heaven and on earth" upon Jesus (Matt. 28:18). That authority was transmitted to the emperor directly, beginning with Constantine; for Christ the King had elected to exercise his sovereignty over the world through the emperor, to whom he had appeared in visions. The emperor was "crowned by God," without mediation, even though the patriarch of Constantinople performed the ritual of coronation. But the

power did move in the opposite direction, for at the consecration of the patriarch the Byzantine emperor would declare: "By the grace of God and by our imperial power, which proceeds from the grace of God, this man is appointed patriarch of Constantinople." The emperor Justinian was said to be Melchizedek, king and priest at the same time (Gen. 14:18).

The dedication of the rebuilt city of Byzantium as Constantinople or New Rome on 11 May 330 was the result, among other things, of Constantine's resolve to reunite his empire and of his wish to establish a truly Christian capital to replace the pagan capital of Old Rome. But when the capital left Rome for Constantinople, there was much of the aura of Rome that it could not export but that devolved, as it had already been doing, on the bishop of Rome. In a scene immortalized by Raphael and then by Verdi, Pope Leo I in 452 confronted Attila, king of the Huns, at Mantua and persuaded him not to lay siege to Rome; he also saved the city from other barbarian conquerors. In that setting, the political implications of the authority of Christ the King came to mean something quite different in Old Rome from what they meant in New Rome. To Peter as the first pope, Christ entrusted the authority to "bind and loose"—to bind and loose sins, but also, so the interpretation eventually ran, to bind and loose political authority.

The coronation of Charlemagne as emperor by Pope Leo III on Christmas Day 800 at Saint Peter's in Rome became the model of how in the West political sovereignty was believed to have passed: from God to Christ, from Christ to the apostle Peter, from Peter to his successors on the "throne of Peter," and from them to emperors and kings. That theory of the political kingship of Christ would be opposed, in the name both of the autonomy of the political order and of the eternal kingship of Christ, by various thinkers of the later Middle Ages, including Dante Alighieri.

"So you are a king?" Pilate had asked Jesus, and in the inscription on the cross he had called him one. But even when they celebrated the kingship of Jesus in the triumphalism of the Byzantine emperor or of the Roman bishop, those who professed obedience to him were obliged to consider the fuller implications of that encounter between Jesus the King and Pontius Pilate the king's procurator (John 18:37–38): "Pilate said to him, 'So you are a king?' Jesus answered, 'You say that I am a king. For this I was born, and for this I have come into the world, to bear witness to the truth. Every one who is of the truth hears my voice.' Pilate said to him, 'What is truth?'" That question has likewise called forth a great variety of answers through the centuries, all of them suggested by the figure of Jesus.

But now was turning my desire and will,

Even as a wheel that equally is moved,

The Love which moves the sun and the other stars.

—*Dante Alighieri,* Paradiso

   (tr. Henry Wadsworth Longfellow)

5 ✤ The Cosmic Christ

The modern scientific belief that "every detailed occurrence can be correlated with its antecedents in a perfectly definite manner, exemplifying general principles," Alfred North Whitehead once suggested, "must come from the medieval insistence on the rationality of God, conceived of as the personal energy of Jehovah and with the rationality of a Greek philosopher." That combination, celebrated by Dante in these closing lines of the *Divine Comedy,* was epitomized in the doctrine of the incarnate Logos.

By the fourth century it had become evident that of all the various titles of majesty for Christ during the first generations, none was to have more momentous consequences than Logos, consequences as momentous for the history of thought as were those of King for the history of politics. One Christian

In the Divine Comedy, *Dante's closing affirmation of "the Love which moves the sun and the other stars" locates the individual experience of the pilgrim and the collective faith of the church in an all-embracing vision of the ultimate harmony of the cosmos with its Creator. This Venetian interpretation of the words from a few cantos earlier in the* Divine Comedy, *"the Mind Divine, wherein is kindled / The Love that turns it, and the power it rains," makes the Cosmic Christ the center of the All.*

At the upper left of this composite icon (opposite page) is the figure of Basil the Great (d. 379), bishop of Caesarea. As the author of a commentary on the creation account in Genesis 1, he strove to harmonize his Christocentric cosmology with the best scientific knowledge of his day. The credibility of that harmonization was enhanced by his enormous prestige as the exponent of the orthodox doctrine of the Trinity and as the systematizer of Eastern Christian monasticism. Among the arts placed into the service of Christ by the newly adopted religion of the Christian Roman empire, none was more pervasive or important than rhetoric, at which two bishops of Constantinople were especially adept: John Chrysostom (d. 407) and his predecessor Gregory of Nazianzus (d. 389), who also appear in this icon. Gregory was surnamed "the Theologian" because of his eloquent defense of the doctrine of the Trinity.

philosopher of that century could speak about "the titles of the Logos, which are so many, so sublime, and so great," attaching all the other titles as predicates to this one. Near the beginning of Goethe's *Faust* the aged philosopher ponders John 1:1 and tries out several translations for it: "In the beginning was the word/the mind/the power/the deed." The term *Logos* can have any and all of those meanings, and many others besides, such as "reason" or "structure" or "purpose." The identification of Jesus as Logos made intellectual, philosophical, and scientific history, for by applying this title to Jesus, the Christian philosophers of the fourth and fifth centuries were enabled to interpret him as the Cosmic Christ.

Those opening words of the Gospel of John were evidently a paraphrase of the opening words of the Book of Genesis, "In the beginning God created the heavens and the

"All things were made through the Word of God, who became flesh in Jesus Christ," the opening verses of the Gospel of John declared, "and without him was not anything made that was made" (John 1:3). Taking that word "all" with the utmost seriousness, Christian artists and thinkers represented rocks and beasts and stars—as well as human beings—as the handiwork of the Cosmic Christ.

earth. . . . And God said" (Gen. 1:1, 3). Because the speaking of God (which is one way to translate *Logos*) made the world possible, it was also the speaking of God that made the world intelligible: Jesus Christ as Logos was the *Word of God* revealing the way and will of God to the world. As the medium of divine revelation, he was also the agent of divine revelation about the cosmos and its creation. His credibility was fundamental to all human understanding. From its very beginning, the Christian doctrine of creation, even of creation through the Logos who was to become incarnate in Jesus, was one on which both divine revelation and human reason were thought to have something valid to say. The interaction between these two ways of knowing as harmony or as contradiction has helped to shape the history not only of theology but of philosophy and science, and it still does. For most of these fourth-century thinkers, what bound together the religious-theological cosmogony of the Nicene Creed ("We believe in one God, Maker of heaven and earth and of all that is—visible and invisible") and the philosophical-scientific cosmogony of Plato and later Platonism was the further affirmation of the content of the Logos doctrine (though the term *Logos* itself did not appear in the Nicene Creed) when it declared that "through the one Lord Jesus Christ, the Son of God, all things were made." That affirmation, however, also drew the line where the two ways of perceiving cosmic reality diverged.

The test case for the relation between them was the definition of creation as "creation out of nothing." That definition was directed against the idea that matter was eternal, hence coeternal with the Creator. According to Basil of Caesarea, although "the philosophers of Greece have made much ado to explain nature," the best they could manage was "some imagination, but no clear comprehension" of that "hidden doctrine" of the Book of Genesis, which had been revealed by the Word of God to and through Moses. And the

The confession of the Cosmic Christ was also a way of affirming the continuity of creation and salvation in the Word, the Logos. "All things were made through him, and without him was not anything made that was made. . . . And the Word became flesh and dwelt among us" (John 1:3, 14). An exemplar of medieval internationalism, the Canterbury Psalter *from the Bibliothèque Nationale, Paris, based on a Psalter from Utrecht, uses its twelve panels to carry the viewer through that continuity of creation and salvation in Christ.*

Word that God spoke, as well as the One to whom God spoke the words, "Let *us* make man in *our* image" (Gen. 1:26), was none other than "his Co-operator, the one through whom [God] created all orders of existence, the one who upholds the universe by his word of power," Jesus Christ the Logos, seen as the second person of the Trinity and the Cosmic Christ. But it was necessary to clarify whether the Word that God spoke at creation, the Logos now present in Jesus, could say, "The Lord *created* me at the beginning of his work" (Prov. 8:22). For then the Logos would be only a creature and part of the order of creation. It was the conclusion of the bitter debates over the doctrine of the Trinity during the fourth century that the Logos as the Word of God spoken at the creation had been with God before the creation, from eternity, and was therefore coeternal, "one in being [*homoousios*] with the Father."

But "Logos of God" when applied to Jesus Christ meant far more than "Word of God," more even than divine revelation; there were many other Greek vocables that would have expressed that much and no more. Employing the specific name *Logos* implied that what had come in Jesus Christ was also the *Reason and Mind of the cosmos.* "There never was a time when God was without the Logos," orthodox thought insisted, "or when he was not the Father." As Christian philosophers pondered the deeper connotations of this identification of Jesus as eternal Logos, the cosmological import of Logos as Reason in the framework of the doctrine of creation became apparent.

Asking the rhetorical question "In what then does the greatness of man consist?" Gregory of Nyssa answered that it consisted "in his being in the image of the Creator." Then he analyzed the connotations of that doctrine for the relation of Christ to the creation: "If you examine the other points by which the divine beauty is expressed, you will find that in them too the likeness in the image [of God] which we present is perfectly preserved. The Godhead is mind and word; for 'in the beginning was the Word,' and the followers of Paul have 'the mind of Christ' which 'speaks' in them. Humanity too is not far removed from these; for you see in yourself word and understanding, which are an imitation of that authentic Mind and Word [namely, Christ as Logos]." There was, therefore, an analogy between the Logos of God, which had become incarnate in Jesus, and the logos of humanity, which was incarnate in each person and perceptible to each person from within. But since the Logos of God, related to the Father as word was to mind, was the divine Demiurge, through whom all of the cosmos had come into being, it followed that "this name [Logos] was given to him because he exists in all things that are."

From this description of the relation between the cosmos as the creation of God and the Logos as the Reason of God there followed two implications for the theory of knowledge. On one hand, it was a countervailing force against the tendency to revel in the paradox of faith in Christ and to glorify the irrational. Although Tertullian never quite said what is often attributed to him, *Credo quia absurdum,* "I believe it because it is absurd," he did say: "The Son of God died; this is by all means to be believed, because it makes no sense [*quia ineptum est*]. And he was buried and rose again; this fact is certain, because it is impossible." Elsewhere he said, "After possessing Christ Jesus, we want no curious disputation, no inquiries after enjoying the gospel! What has Athens to do with Jerusalem?"

Taken by themselves as literal and authoritative, such sentiments would have brought an end to philosophical thought and would have aborted scientific investigation, both of which depend on the assumption that there is a rational order in the cosmos. But by the latter half of the fourth century it had become possible for those who still accepted the paradox of faith in Christ to affirm nevertheless the validity of the rational process and to appeal to the evidence of "our very eyes and the law of nature." For a creation that had been carried out by God the Father through his eternal Son the Logos could not be arbitrary or haphazard, nor could it be "conceived by chance and without reason"; it had to have "a useful end." It was a fundamental difference between humanity and other creatures that, having been created in the image of God and by a special action of the creating Logos, even the human body must be *logikos,* which meant "capable of speech" or "suited to the use of reason" or in any case "mirroring forth the presence of the creating Logos."

This confidence was, however, restrained from presumption by the other pole of the dialectic: a profound sense, also based on the revelation in Christ, of the limitations that had been placed on the human capacity to understand ultimate reality. As happened so often, a Christian heretic was the catalyst for a fundamental insight when he allegedly claimed that he could know the essence of God as well as God himself did. His orthodox opponents made a point of declaring that there was much about God that they could not know. For an investigation of creatures, it was enough to know their "names" in order to understand their "essences," but "the uncreated nature [of God] alone, which we acknowledge in the Father and in the Son and in the Holy Spirit, transcends all significance of names." For "the Deity cannot be expressed in words"; rather, "we sketch It by Its attributes" and so "obtain a certain faint and feeble and partial idea concerning It." The outcome was expressed in the motto of the fourth-century Latin theologian Hilary of Poitiers: "God is to be believed insofar as he speaks of himself." And God had spoken decisively in the Logos, incarnate in the historical flesh of Jesus Christ. Thus the cosmos was reliably knowable and at the same time it remained mysterious, both of these because the Logos was the Mind and Reason of God.

Because the Logos incarnate in Jesus was the Reason of God, it was also possible to see the Logos as the very *Structure of the universe.* Combining the account of creation in Genesis with the Platonic doctrine of Forms, Basil of Caesarea provided a graphic description of that structure: "Before all those things which now attract our notice existed, God, after casting about in his mind and determining to bring into being that which had no being, imagined the world such as it ought to be, and created matter in harmony with the form which he wished to give it. . . . He welded all the diverse parts of the cosmos by links of indissoluble attachment and established between them so perfect a fellowship and harmony that the most distant, in spite of their distance, appeared united in one universal sympathy." That harmony, binding the atom and the galaxy, was expressed in a cosmic *systēma*, all of it brought about by the "magnificence of the Creator-Logos." The concept of harmony in the universe expressed in the Greek word *systēma* also hovered over one of the most powerful of the New Testament statements about the Cosmic Christ, in whom "all things hold together [or: are made into a cosmic system, *synestēken*]" (Col. 1:17).

The identification of the Creator-Logos in Jesus as the foundation for the very structure of the universe had its basis in the even more fundamental identification of the Logos as the *Agent of creation out of nothing,* or out of "nonbeing." The Creator could be described as "the one who is [*ho ōn*]," but creatures had their being only by participation in the Creator. In the fullest sense, therefore, only the Creator could be said "to be." For the same reason, using the name Father for God was *not* a figure of speech. Only because God was the Father of the Logos-Son and "the Father, from whom every fatherhood, in heaven and on earth, is named" (Eph. 3:14–15) could the term *father* also be applied to human parents, and that *was* a figure of speech; for all human parents were children of other parents. That was also why the Logos could not be a creature, not even the primary creature; for all creatures had been brought out of nonbeing, and as the agent who had brought them out of nonbeing the Creator-Logos must "have being" in the full and nonmetaphorical sense of the word.

Created out of nonbeing, the cosmos manifested in its "order and providence" the ordering presence of "the Logos of God who is over all and who governs all." The universe was not "absurd," that is, "bereft of the Logos," but made sense because of the Logos. Conversely, its hold on reality was derived from its hold on the Logos, without whom it would slip back into nonbeing: "God guides [the universe] by the Logos, so that by the direction, providence, and ordering of the Logos, the creation may be illumined and enabled to abide always securely." Because sin was a turning of the eyes away from God and from the Logos, sinners were threatened with falling back into the abyss of nonbeing out of which the creating action of the Logos had called them. To overcome this threat, the Logos, as the *Savior of the cosmos,* became incarnate in Jesus Christ, who rose from the dead victorious over sin, death, and hell. This was necessary because the world that the Logos had fashioned was now a fallen world. It was characteristic of these Greek Christian philosophers that, by contrast with the individualism sometimes manifest especially in Western theology, they always viewed humanity and cosmos in proximity. Not only did "all things hold together" in Christ the Logos as the Structure of the cosmos, but it would also be in the Logos as Savior that "the universe itself is to be freed from the shackles of mortality and enter upon the liberty and splendor of the children of God."

It is helpful here to distinguish between those philosophical theologies that have interpreted death as the result of guilt and those that have tended to see death as the conse-

In the Eastern Christian
tradition, the descent of Divinity
into human flesh in the incarnation
of the Logos, the Cosmic Christ, had
as its ultimate goal and result the
empowerment of men and women
to attain nothing short of becoming
"partakers of the divine nature"
(2 Peter 1:4). An early icon and a
twentieth-century painting (opposite page) of the Transfiguration of
Christ both depict that event (Matt.
17:1–8) as the anticipation of that
participation in the divine nature
and "deification" of humanity
achieved through the
incarnation.

quence of transiency; neither emphasis exists utterly without echoes of the other, but the distinction is clear. If sin was defined as a relapse into the nothingness out of which the creating Logos had taken humanity, it was appropriate to describe the plight of the human soul as "imagining evil for itself" and therefore as supposing that "it is doing something" when, by committing the sin that is nonbeing, "it is in fact doing nothing." This total reversal of the created metaphysical polarity between being and nonbeing was the meaning of the fall. The fall both of humanity and of the world was a loss of the tenuous hold on true being and therefore a relapse into the abyss. In the case of humanity, it was all the more tragic because only Adam and Eve among all creatures had been created in the image of God.

The corollary of this view was an understanding of the saving activity of Jesus the Logos as not only expiation of guilt but also repair of the fracture in being caused by alienation from the God who was defined as "the one who is." By becoming incarnate in Jesus, the Logos enabled human beings to transcend themselves and to "become partakers of the divine nature" (2 Pet. 1:4). "The Logos of God has become human," one Greek church father after another would say, "so that you might learn from a human being how a human being may become divine." The original creation in the image of God had been brought about through the Logos, and would now achieve not only restoration but consummation and perfection through the same Logos: his incarnation would achieve our deification. And the whole cosmos would have its proper share in that consummation; for "the establishment of the church is a re-creation of the world," in which "the Logos has created a multitude of stars," a new heaven and a new earth. From the ascription of the creation of the universe to Jesus the Logos it also followed that the Logos was the *Goal of the cosmos,* Omega as well as Alpha. The observation that time moved along in sequence should lead to the recognition that time would also have an end, just as it had had a beginning. As the Goal of the cosmos, the Logos represented, to some of these thinkers, the hope that even the devil could finally be restored to wholeness in "the restitution of all things, and with the reformation of the world humanity also shall be changed from the transient and the earthly to the incorruptible and the eternal."

All these metaphysical constructs of fourth-century Christian philosophers about the preexistent Word and Logos were said to find their religious and moral focus, and even their intellectual justification, in the historical figure of Jesus in the Gospels, in "the humble Word," and in "the glory of his passion" on the cross. "In the beginning was the Word": this was taught by many thinkers who had never heard of Jesus of Nazareth. But what made the portrait of the Logos as Cosmic Christ special was the declaration that the Word had become flesh in Jesus and that in Jesus the incarnate Word had suffered and died on the cross and had risen from the dead. Yet if that declaration was true, there was ultimately no way to avoid declaring as well that nothing short of the cosmos was the object of the love that had come through him. For "God so loved the world that he gave his only Son, that whoever believes in him should not perish but have eternal life" (John 3:16). The "whoever" could indeed be taken to mean each individual, one at a time; but the Greek word for "world" in this passage was still *kosmos*.

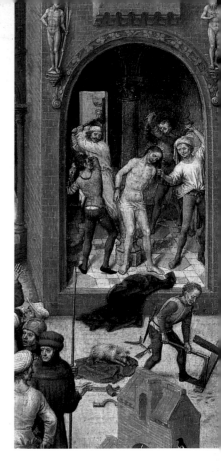

Of man's first disobedience, and the fruit

Of that forbidden tree, whose mortal taste

Brought death into the world, and all our woe,

With loss of Eden, till one greater Man

Restore us, and regain the blissful seat. . . .

—John Milton, Paradise Lost

6 ✤ The Son of Man

It is evident from the Gospels that Jesus' favorite designation for himself was "the Son of Man." In the Hebrew Bible the term was sometimes a way of referring to humanity, with the meaning "mortal man" (Ps. 8:4). But in later Judaism, as also in the sayings of Jesus, it acquired apocalyptic connotations: "As the lightning comes from the east and shines as far as the west, so will be the coming of the Son of man. . . . All the tribes of the earth will mourn, and they will see the Son of man coming on the clouds of heaven with power and great glory" (Matt. 24:27, 30). After the New Testament the title regained its original significance, referring to the human nature of Jesus, in parallel with "Son of God," referring to his divine nature.

Although Jesus had from the very beginning been seen by his followers as

When *"Jesus came out, wearing the crown of thorns and the purple robe, Pilate said to them, 'Behold the man!'"* (John 19:5). With these words Pontius Pilate was referring to the figure of Jesus as the Man of Sorrows, despised and rejected (Isa. 53:3), which is how artists (including the Master of the Bruges Passion Scenes in the early sixteenth century) have captured the scene. The words "Behold the man!" may also be applied to Jesus as the revelation of the mystery of the nature of humanity, the Representative Man.

the disclosure of the mystery of the nature of divinity, they came to recognize, as their reflection on him deepened, that he was also the revelation of the mystery of the nature of humanity; in the formula of the Second Vatican Council, "Only in the mystery of the incarnate Word does the mystery of man take on light." Logically it might seem that it should have been the other way around: diagnosis should have preceded prescription, with the doctrine of the fall of man coming first, to be followed by the doctrine of the person and work of Christ as the divine answer to the human predicament. But historically that was not how it developed, for the position of Jesus as the Son of God, the Logos, and the Cosmic Christ had to be clarified first, before there could come a mature understanding of the human predicament. Rather than making the punishment fit the crime, Christian thought had to gauge the magnitude of human sin by first taking the measure of the one on whom the divine punishment of the cross had been imposed; thus the diagnosis was made to fit the prescription. In John Milton's noble language, only the coming of the "one greater Man [to] restore us, and regain the blissful seat" could make painfully obvious the full implications "of man's first disobedience, and the fruit of that forbidden tree, whose mortal taste brought death into the world, and all our woe, with loss of Eden."

The definition of how it was that the coming of the light should have proved to be the revelation of darkness was the historic achievement of Augustine of Hippo, who died a century after the Council of Nicaea. The historical reasons for this sequence are complex, not least among them being the intellectual and religious development of Augustine himself. But within and behind them is a reason within the human predicament, as formulated with characteristic precision and verve by a disciple of Augustine twelve centuries later, the French scientist and Christian philosopher Blaise Pascal, who died in 1662: "The knowledge of God without that of man's misery causes pride. The knowledge of man's misery without that of God causes despair. The knowledge of Jesus Christ constitutes the middle course, because in him we find both God and our misery." Much of what Augustine said about man's "misery" was his own special insight, but in the use of the figure of Jesus to define the grandeur of humanity he attached himself to the thought of the preceding centuries. In the fullest sense of the word, the true image of God was the man Jesus. Although Augustine sometimes spoke as though the image of God had been altogether obliterated through the fall, he made it clear upon further reflection near the end of his life that the fall was not to be interpreted "as though man had lost everything he had of the image of God." For if the image had been totally destroyed, there would have been no point of contact between human nature as such and the incarnation of the Logos in the truly human nature of Jesus. Jesus was, then, not only the image of divinity, but the image of humanity as it had originally been intended to be and as through him it could now become: "God loves us, such as we shall be, not such as we [now] are." The contours of this future condition were already visible, not in our empirical humanity but in the humanity of Jesus, the Word made flesh; and as it viewed that prospect, empirical human

The climax of the creation narrative in the Book of Genesis, and therefore the climax of Michelangelo's monumental portrayal of the creation on the ceiling of the Sistine Chapel, came when "God created man in his own image, in the image of God he created him; male and female he created them" (Gen. 1:27). Of course, this could not be a literal physical resemblance of a God who cannot be seen, but the "image of God" became a way of identifying the qualities that made human beings distinctively human, as those qualities were seen above all in the humanity of Jesus Christ.

nature was filled with yearning and with a desire to press forward toward that ideal. Thus "Christ Jesus is the Mediator between God and men, not insofar as he is divine but insofar as he is human," as not only the source but also the "goal, of all perfection."

Augustine acknowledged that he had had difficulty making the transition from the "immutability of the Logos, which I knew as well as I could and about which I did not have any doubts at all" (and which one did not have to be a Christian to accept, as the teachings of Neoplatonism proved) to the full meaning of the words of the Gospel of John, "The Logos was made flesh," which he had come to understand "only somewhat later." But once he did understand these words, the Logos made flesh, whose humility was made known in the narratives of the Gospels, dominated his language about Christ. It was from the portrait of the Logos in the Gospel of John that Augustine developed his most speculative and most sublime psychological insight into the image of God: it was an image of the Trinity. He investigated the various "traces of the Trinity," the ways in which the human mind by its very structure as single and yet possessing relationship within itself, as one and yet three, could be interpreted as a reflection of the relation between Father, Son, and Holy Spirit. One of these "traces of the Trinity" was the trinity of being, knowledge, and will, capacities that were distinct within the mind and yet were one mind: "for I am, and I know, and I will." Again, "When I . . . love anything, there are three realities involved: myself, and the beloved, and the love itself." Perhaps the most profound was the analogy of "memory, understanding, and will," which "are not three lives but one life, not three minds but one mind" and yet not identical. Augustine freely conceded the inadequacy, and obviously sensed the artificiality, of all such constructs, including the very language of the ecclesiastical doctrine of the Trinity itself (which was necessary if faith was not to remain altogether silent, but which could not pretend to provide an accurate description of the mystery of the inner life of God). But this much was certain: Jesus Christ was for Augustine the key to the mystery of the Trinity and through it the key to the mystery of the human mind.

Profound and provocative though this exploration of the psychological analogies to the Trinity in the human mind may have been, Augustine's most important contribution to the history of human psychology came in his doctrine of sin. Walter Lippmann was re-

So massive has been the influence of Augustine of Hippo on the history of Christian thought and spirituality, especially in the West, that he has been called "the second founder of the faith," a title for which he would not seem to have a serious rival. An altarpiece by Michael Pacher from about 1483 associates him with Pope Gregory the Great (and, on other panels, with Ambrose of Milan and Jerome).

To an extent that has seldom been matched, Augustine was a master of biblical interpretation in his writings, a metaphysician whose speculations ranged across the celestial and terrestrial spheres, and a bishop and pastor who put all his talents into the service of Christ and the church—all three at the same time. Sandro Botticelli wove these three together by depicting him with his books, an armillary sphere, and a miter.

ferring above all to this doctrine when in the fateful year of 1941 he was moved to reflect on the presence within human nature of what he called "ice-cold evil." "The modern skeptical world," he wrote, "has been taught for some 200 years a conception of human nature in which the reality of evil, so well known to the ages of faith, has been discounted. Almost all of us grew up in an environment of such easy optimism that we can scarcely know what is meant, though our ancestors knew it well, by the satanic will. We shall have to recover this forgotten but essential truth—along with so many others that we lost when, thinking we were enlightened and advanced, we were merely shallow and blind."

What role did the figure of Jesus play in this Augustinian explanation of human nature? The most fundamental component in any answer to that question is to be sought in an assessment of his *Confessions,* which is, from the first sentence to the last, one long prayer of "confession," defined as the accusation of oneself and the praise of God. Augustine could speak with as much candor as he did here because the sin he was confessing was the sin that God in Christ had forgiven. He was expressing the "sacrifice of my confessions" in the presence of a God whose eye could penetrate into even the most closed of hearts, to whom therefore it was not possible to lie. But he was also expressing the "confession of a broken and contrite heart" in the presence of a God whose grace "through Jesus Christ our Lord" had granted him deliverance from the power of sin and to whom therefore it was not necessary to lie. In a series of apostrophes to Christ scattered throughout the *Confessions,* Augustine gave devotional expression to what he asserted and defended elsewhere as dogma, as "my faith because it is also the Catholic faith": that Jesus Christ was the Son of God, the source of grace, the ground of hope, and the worthy object of prayer, adoration, and confession.

Augustine focused his attention on various sins of his youth, at least two of which have achieved considerable psychological notoriety. One of these was being "in love with loving" but not knowing the true nature of love. As T. S. Eliot paraphrases Augustine's words,

> To Carthage then I came
> Burning burning burning burning
> O Lord Thou pluckest me out
> O Lord Thou pluckest
> burning.

If lust is defined, in keeping with both the Hebrew Bible and the New Testament, not as natural sexual desire but as the tendency to regard another person as primarily a sex object to be used, Augustine's probing of the hidden fires of sexuality begins to seem considerably less quaint than it may at first appear. Alongside the undeniable extremes to which he often went in his language about sexual desire even within the boundaries of matrimony, he was at the same time rejecting the heretical notion that "marriage and for-

The intellectual and spiritual
odyssey of Augustine took him from
paganism to Christianity, from
Neoplatonic philosophy to Catholic
theology, from heresy to orthodoxy.
It is as the thinker and the scholar
that the Venetian Vittore Carpaccio
interpreted him in a painting from
ca. 1500, surrounded by his library
and with his pen poised ready to
write still another of the books, such
as the Confessions and the City
of God, that have shaped all
subsequent generations.

nication are two evils, of which the second is worse," and substituting for it the orthodox Catholic principle that "marriage and continence are two goods, of which the second is better," which did have warrant in the teachings of Jesus (Matt. 19:12) and of Paul (1 Cor. 7:1–5), as well as in those of noble pagans. The clinching argument in favor of the holiness of marriage came for Augustine from the words of Paul (Eph. 5:25, 32): "Husbands, love your wives, as Christ loved the church and gave himself up for her. . . . This is a great sacrament [*magnum sacramentum,* in the Latin translation], and I take it to mean Christ and the church." Marriage was a sacrament of Christ and the church.

The other youthful sin mentioned in the *Confessions* that has provoked great psychological interest is his anecdote of stealing fruit from a pear tree. Augustine's recollection of the incident gave him an opportunity to probe the mysterious depths of the motivation of evil acts. The pears were not particularly attractive to him, nor did he find them very good to eat; he did not need them. What he did need was to steal them, and having satisfied that need, he threw the fruit to the pigs. When he speaks of having thereby "become to myself an unfruitful land," he is, in his characteristic allegorical fashion, echoing the story of the fruit of the tree in the Garden of Eden.

Augustine rejected indignantly any suggestion that he was merely extrapolating from his personal views and experiences and generalizing these into a universal condition. Rather, he was seeking to take account of a recognizable universal condition. For if every person was exactly poised between good and evil, as Augustine's opponents seemed to be claiming, how could one account for the statistical regularity with which every person made the same choice that Adam and Eve had made, in favor of sin and against the good? This was not to deny that there could be "on earth righteous men, great men—brave, prudent, chaste, patient, pious, merciful"; yet even they could not be "without sin." Who was more holy than the saints and apostles? "And yet the Lord [Jesus] prescribed to them to say in their prayer, 'Forgive us our debts' (Matt. 6:12)," which proved that they, too, were sinners.

There was only one unqualified exception to the rule, Jesus Christ as the Mediator between a righteous God and a sinful humanity. His status as the sinless Savior proved the necessity of salvation, and anyone who denied the universality of sin was obliged, for the sake of consistency, to deny the universality of the salvation and mediation accomplished in him. This was for Augustine the decisive argument in his analysis of the human condition. For all "ordinary" people, death was not only universal but involuntary: there might be some choice about whether to die at this time or that time but no choice about whether to die or not to die. The exception was Jesus Christ, who was not mortal by nature but who "died for mortals" and therefore was the only one who could say of himself: "I lay down my life, that I may take it again. No one takes it from me, but I lay it down of my own accord" (John 10:17–18). Augustine's most influential insight into human nature

and psychology, the idea of original sin, was therefore not only a way of speaking about the misery of humanity but a means of recognizing and praising the uniqueness of Jesus.

In spite of the sensitivity of the introspection in the *Confessions,* Augustine would not have gained this insight without the illumination of Christ, reasoning backward from the cure to the diagnosis. Further substantiation for that hypothesis comes from his use of the Virgin Birth, from which he concluded that because Jesus "alone could be born in such a way as not to need to be reborn," all those who were born in the normal way, as the result of the sexual union of their parents, were in need of being reborn in Christ through baptism. The statement of the Psalmist "Behold, I was brought forth in iniquity, and in

Unlike the sacraments of baptism and the Eucharist, marriage was not instituted by Jesus while he was on earth but had been instituted already in the Garden of Eden by the Creator. Nevertheless it happens to be the only one of the seven "sacraments" of the church to be designated as such in the Latin New Testament (Eph. 5:32). In Gerard David's Marriage at Cana *from the early sixteenth century (opposite page), the presence of Jesus (John 2:1–11) consecrates this marriage, and with it all marriage, making it a sacrament of Christ and the church.*

When John Milton in the opening lines of Paradise Lost *spoke of "the fruit / Of that forbidden tree, whose mortal taste / Brought death into the world," he was summarizing many centuries' worth of controversy (as in Augustine's works) and art (as in the missal of the archbishop of Salzburg, from 1481), dealing with typology between the death-giving tree in the Garden of Eden and the life-giving tree of the cross of Jesus.*

By consigning all human beings born of the natural union between man and woman to the "mass of perdition" stained by original sin, Augustine's comprehensive language seemed to collide with the long-standing language of Christian devotion and theology about the Virgin Mary. But he hastened to reassure his readers: "We must except the Holy Virgin Mary, concerning whom I wish to raise no question when it touches the subject of sins, out of honor to the Lord." Murillo's painting of the Immaculate Conception celebrates her as that one exception.

sin did my mother conceive me" (Ps. 51:5) was spoken in the awareness of forgiveness through the "selfsame faith" in Christ that was now confessed by the Catholic church. That was why Augustine entitled the treatise just quoted *On the Grace of Christ and Original Sin:* the knowledge of the grace of Christ was unintelligible without the knowledge of original sin, but the knowledge of original sin was unbearable without a knowledge of the grace of Christ.

There was, however, one additional exception that he had to consider: Mary the Virgin Mother of Jesus. After rejecting the contention that various other saints, both male and female, had been totally sinless, Augustine continued: "We must except the Holy Virgin Mary, concerning whom I wish to raise no question when it touches the subject of sins, *out of honor to the Lord;* for from him we know what abundance of grace for overcoming sin in every particular was conferred upon her who had the merit to conceive and to bear him who undoubtedly had no sin." The outcome of that exception was to have a profound effect not only on devotion and theology but on art and literature for the next fifteen centuries. Yet only in 1854 did Pope Pius IX make the doctrine binding that, "in view of the merits of Christ Jesus, the Savior of the [entire] human race," which included her, Mary had been permitted to become an exception to the universality of original sin.

"Know thyself" was a motto carved on the temple of the oracle at Delphi. As the linking of the Delphic oracle and the prophet Isaiah suggests, others before Augustine had applied that axiom, often attributing it to Socrates, to the need for a self-understanding in the light of Christ. Augustine's knowledge of himself had grown out of his existential needs but had led him to Jesus, "the humble Word," and to "the glory of his passion." Here alone he was able to confront, to understand, and to articulate those needs, for the Jesus of Augustine was the key to what humanity was and to what, through Jesus, it could become.

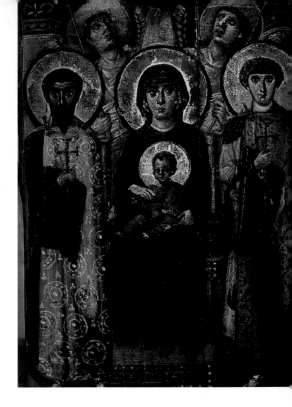

Flesh fade, and mortal trash
Fall to the residuary worm; world's wildfire, leave but ash:
  In a flash, at a trumpet crash,
I am all at once what Christ is, since he was what I am, and
This Jack, joke, poor potsherd, patch, matchwood,
  immortal diamond,
  Is immortal diamond.
—*Gerard Manley Hopkins*
  That Nature Is a Heraclitean Fire

7 ✢ The True Image

The victory of Jesus Christ over the gods of Greece and Rome in the fourth century did not, as both friend and foe might have expected, bring about the demise of religious art; on the contrary, it was responsible over the next fifteen centuries for a massive and magnificent outpouring of creativity that is probably without parallel in the entire history of art. How and why did that happen? How could Jesus have evolved from the very antithesis of all representations of the divine in images to become their most important concrete inspiration—and eventually their principal theoretical justification?

In the Ten Commandments, whose permanent validity Christians also accepted, the prohibition of religious art as idolatrous was explicit and comprehensive: "You shall not make for yourself a graven image, or any likeness of anything that is in heaven above, or that is in the earth beneath, or that is in the water under the earth" (Ex. 20:4). Quoting such prohibitions from the Hebrew Bible as well as the opinions of such pagan thinkers as Cicero that "the deities which men worshiped were false," the followers of Jesus claimed to be joining themselves both to Judaism and to the best in classical paganism when they rejected images, but they chided enlightened pagans for allowing the "vulgar and ignorant" to keep their images. What was more, they went beyond Judaism in denouncing as well the very notion of religious architecture: "The God who made the world and everything in it, being Lord of heaven and earth, does not live in shrines made by man" (Acts 17:24). They took the prohibition of images to apply not only to the idolaters who worshiped them but even to the artists who made them by practicing a "deceptive art." Thus in contradistinction to paganism and in some ways even to Judaism, they claimed, in the name of the revelation of the divine that had come in Jesus, to be proclaiming a God who transcended all efforts of human hands to devise sacred images; for it was the rational soul that was the "image of God." There were neither sacred images nor sacred places; not even the places where Jesus had been born and buried were possessed of any special holiness.

Only with the challenge to the use of images in the eighth and ninth centuries were the orthodox Byzantine interpreters of the person and message of Jesus compelled to articulate a comprehensive philosophical and theological aesthetic based on the person of Christ, an aesthetic within which the legitimacy of drawing images of the divine would take its proper place. Fundamental to that aesthetic was the unanimous affirmation of the New Testament and the early church that, in a special and unique sense, "the image of God is his Logos." That assumption was shared by the proponents of both major alternatives in the controversies over images, but from it they drew diametrically opposed conclusions.

The earliest application of this assumption to the question of religious art came from the opponents of images. When Constantia, sister of the emperor Constantine, wrote to Eusebius of Caesarea requesting an image of Christ, he replied: "I do not know what has impelled you to command that an image of our Savior be drawn. Which image of Christ do you want? Is it to be a true and unchangeable one, portraying his countenance truly, or is it to be the one which he assumed on our behalf when he took on the appearance of the 'form of a slave' (Phil. 2:7)?" To Eusebius the countenance of Christ in the form of a slave was transitory and not permanently relevant—even though, presumably, an eyewitness in Jerusalem who saw Jesus in the flesh during the first century could have drawn such a picture. But that would not have been "a true image" of the one who was himself the True Image. For Eusebius, a "true" image of that Image would have to be unchangeable, for only that would "portray his countenance truly." And such an image was, by definition, impossible.

In applying the concept of Christ as Image, the iconoclasts of the eighth and ninth

Western Christian art no less than Eastern would have been impossible if the eighth-century campaign against religious images had been successful, but it was in the Byzantine East that the defense of Christian art was waged and in the worship and art of the many Orthodox centers represented in this chapter that the icons were vindicated. Because Christ was God Almighty, Maker and Ruler of all (Pantocrator), the "Redeemer and Source of Life," now in human form and therefore the True Image, it was permissible, indeed obligatory, to picture him in an image.

centuries—led by Emperors Leo III, Constantine V, and Leo V—invoked the authority of the councils of the fourth and fifth centuries, at which this concept had been definitively formulated. The only way an image of Christ could be a true image was in the same way that Christ himself was the True Image of the Father, "one in being" with the one whom he imaged. Therefore an icon of Christ could not be a true image of him unless it, too, was "one in being" with him. Obviously, no work of art made by human hands—nor even, for that matter, the images supposedly made without hands, by angels—could ever hope to meet such a qualification. The only image of Christ that could be said to be "one in being" with Christ in that same way was the Eucharist. "It has been laid down for us," the iconoclasts taught, "that Christ *is* to be portrayed in an image, but only as the holy teaching transmitted by divine tradition says: 'Do this in remembrance of me.' Therefore

Icons of Christ could take many forms and employ many media. In Ravenna, Italy, as the seat of Byzantine power and administration for the West, Christ was carved in ivory, holding the book of the Gospel and seated between Saints Peter and Paul. The other wing of the diptych has the Virgin Mary in a similar pose between the angels Michael and Gabriel.

it is obviously not permitted to portray him in an image or to carry out a remembrance of him in any other way, since this portrayal [in the Eucharist] is true and this way of portraying is sacred." The Eucharist precluded every other so-called image of Christ.

The Council of Chalcedon in 451 set it down as orthodox dogma that Christ consisted of two natures, divine and human, in a single person. On this basis the opponents of images insisted that Christ, as the True Image of God, was "beyond description, beyond comprehension, beyond change, and beyond measure," because such transcendence was characteristic of God. This rule applied even to the miracles and sufferings of Christ in the days of his flesh, which it was "illegitimate to portray in images." Whatever the status of Christ "before the passion and the resurrection" may have been, however, latter-day artists in any case had no right to attempt to portray him now; for now "the body of Christ is incorruptible, having inherited immortality," and that was beyond the competence of any artistic representation. As Emperor Constantine V at the middle of the eighth century put it, "If someone makes an image of Christ, . . . he has not really penetrated the depths of the dogma of the inseparable union of the two natures of Christ" as formulated by the councils.

Underlying these aspersions on the artistic portrayal of Jesus Christ appears to have been a deep-seated aversion to the material and physical aspects of his person: "It is degrading and demeaning to depict Christ with material representations. For one should confine oneself to the mental observation [of him] . . . through sanctification and righteousness." The portrayal of him in an image inevitably diverted the attention from what was important about him, his transcendent rather than his immanent qualities. The requirement both of the Platonic tradition and of the Gospel of John (4:24), "God is spirit, and those who worship him must worship in spirit and truth," was being violated whenever the outward physical picture was substituted for the spirit and whenever the deception of the icon replaced the truth.

"We join you in declaring that the Son is the Image of God the Father," the defenders of the icons said to the iconoclasts. But the Jesus Christ who was the True Image was the one who had been made human, and thus physical and material, by his incarnation and birth from the Virgin Mary; and therefore a Christian icon was not an idol but an image of the Image: such was in essence the case for a Christian art. The logical implication of the view of Christ set forth in the orthodox tradition was a justification for the representation of Christ in pictures. Who invented images? "God himself was the first" to do so, John of Damascus replied. God was the first and the original image-maker of the universe.

In the most fundamental sense, the Son of God was uniquely the living Image of God (Col. 1:15), "image in his very nature, the image of the invisible Father, differing in no way from him" except by being the Son rather than the Father. The worship of the Son of God was therefore not idolatrous, because, already in the fourth-century formula of Basil of

If, as the defenders of images proved, it was legitimate to draw icons of Christ as the True Image, then by extension it was also legitimate to draw the Virgin Mary as the Mother of God, or Theotokos, through whom he had assumed the human nature that made him visible as the True Image. And the legitimation of icons in Constantinople was extended to other Eastern Orthodox cultures.

Caesarea, "the honor paid to the image [the Son] passes over to the prototype [the Father]." Quite apart from human history, there was, in the very life of the Godhead, an image-making and an image-manifesting, which expressed the mystery of the eternal relation of Father, Son, and Holy Spirit.

In a secondary and derivative sense, image could be taken to refer to the "images and paradigms in God of the things that are to be produced by him." Because God was absolute and unchangeable, with "no variation" (James 1:17), he did not, as the Artist-Maker of the cosmos, create the particulars of the empirical world directly. Instead, creation consisted in the designing of these images and paradigms. Just as a human architect, "before a house is constructed, already images in his mind the scheme and plan of what it is to be," so, before any particular reality came into being as such, it had, as image, been predetermined within the "counsel" of God, and in that sense it already possessed reality. God created the world we see through the Logos, his Image, who in turn called into being the Platonic Forms, the images from which that world would come.

Although the entire created world was in this sense an image of God, or perhaps more precisely an image of the Image of God, the human creature had a special claim to that honorific title. For in the creation story of Genesis, God was said to have created man in his own image. The image of God the Creator in man the creature was an example of an

As it is described in chapter 20 of the Gospel of John, the first encounter of the Risen Christ was not with Peter or John or any of the other apostles but with Mary Magdalene, whom one church father therefore named "apostle to the apostles." At first she did not recognize him, but when he greeted her by name, "she turned and said to him in Hebrew 'Rabboni' (which means Teacher). Jesus said to her, 'Do not hold me, for I have not yet ascended to the Father; but go to my brethren.'"

The suffering and death on the cross were at the opposite end of the earthly ministry of Christ from his baptism, but they, too, were appropriately depicted in icons. Working on the island of Crete in the years immediately following the fall of Constantinople in 1453, Nicholas Tzafuris continued, but also adapted and perhaps "Westernized" somewhat, the Byzantine tradition in showing Christ as the Man of Sorrows (Isa. 53:3).

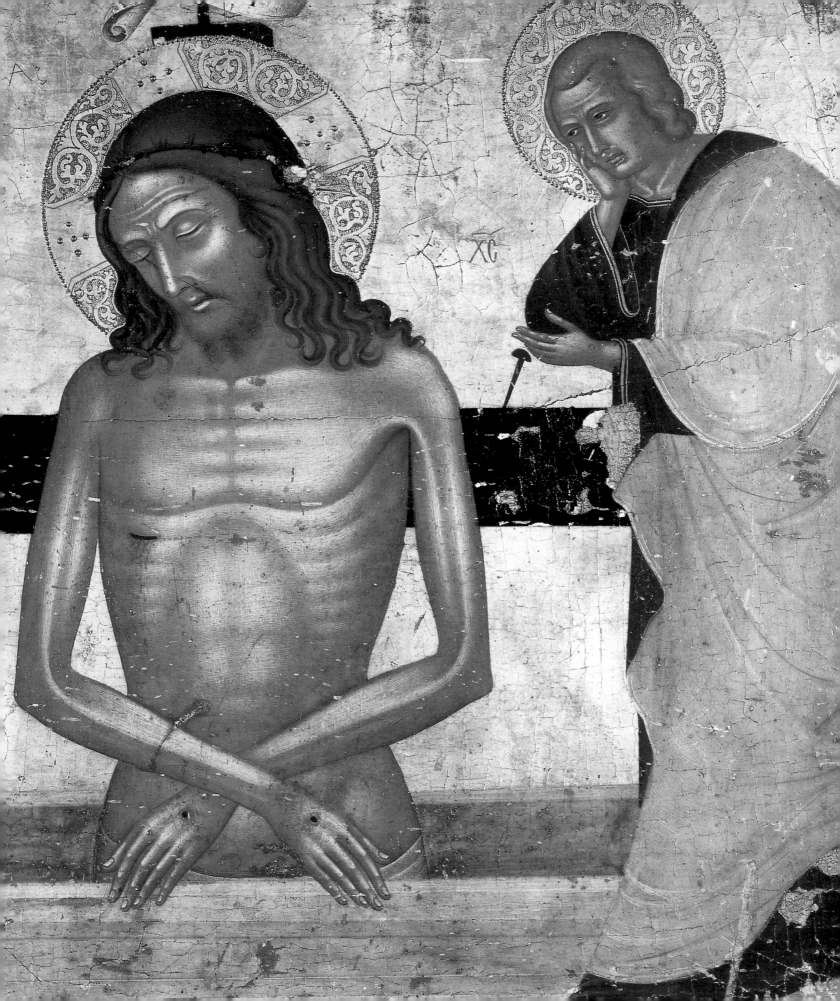

"He descended into hell" is perhaps the most puzzling phrase in the Apostles' Creed. According to the New Testament (1 Pet. 3:18–20), Christ was "put to death in the flesh but made alive in the spirit; in which he went and preached to the spirits in prison, who formerly did not obey." Was this intended to give them a second chance, or was this when "he disarmed the principalities and powers and made a public example of them, triumphing over them in him" (Col. 2:15)? The Eastern emphasis on Christ the Victor, seen also in this sixteenth-century Russian icon (opposite page), gave special force to the latter explanation.

Christ the True Image was also Jesus the Turning Point of History. In both East and West, therefore, the prospect of the Last Judgment was a source of terror and of fascination. Known in Russia as Strashnyj sud, "the terrifying judgment," it inspired artists such as this icon painter from the fifteenth-century Novgorod school to glorify the one before whom all humanity would stand in what was known in the Latin West as the Dies irae, the Day of Wrath.

Emboldened by the use of the incarnation of Christ as a justification for images, Eastern artists were even willing to paint the invisible Holy Trinity—not in the inaccessible reaches of the divine life but in earthly appearances such as the one to Abraham, when "the Lord appeared to him by the oaks of Mamre. . . . He lifted up his eyes and looked, and behold, three men stood in front of him" (Gen. 18:1–2). Andrey Rublyov, who is now a saint of the Russian Orthodox church, visualized the scene in his Old Testament Trinity.

image "by imitation," mirroring forth in the structure of human life and thought the nature of God the image-maker. A living God could not have wood and stone as a fitting image, but only the rational soul of his supreme creature. Hence the command against making images was based not on a degraded view of images but on an exalted one: because a proper image of God could only be something as noble as the human mind, it demeaned both God the image-maker and man the image to attempt to substitute for it some less worthy picture.

In addition to these metaphysical usages of the word *image,* there were historical usages. The human mind could not perceive such spiritual realities as angels without physical images and physical language. The Bible itself had accommodated its ways of speaking to this characteristic of human thought and language, presenting its sublime content by means of simple and even homely analogies and making the "eternal power and deity" of God perceptible "in the things that have been made" (Rom. 1:20). As biblical usage likewise made clear, historical images of this kind could move in either direction within time, describing either "the things that are yet to be in the future" or "the things that have already happened in the past." According to the Christian way of reading it, the Hebrew Bible was filled with images and anticipations of what was to be fulfilled with the coming of Jesus. They were real in and of themselves: Israel did cross the Red Sea during the exodus from Egypt. But they were also images of what was to come: the crossing of the Red Sea was a "type" of Christian baptism. And yet, some images were "monuments of past events, of some wondrous achievement or of some virtue, for glory and honor and remembrance." A book of history written as a memorial of past events was such an image, and nonliterary images of memory were intrinsically no different from books; they were "books for the illiterate," differing from the Bible only in form, not in content.

The gulf between these two categories of images, the metaphysical and the historical, was bridged when the Logos became flesh. The fallacy of misplaced concreteness, by which idolatry had correctly intuited an identity of images in the abstract but had falsely executed it in the concrete, had now been replaced by the concrete events of the life of Jesus described in the Gospels, as recounted by the eighth-century Greek theologian and "Doctor of the Church" John of Damascus in what sounds like a catalogue raisonné of Byzantine icons:

> Because the one who by excellency of nature transcends all quantity and size and magnitude, who has his being in the form of God, has now, by taking upon himself the form of a slave, contracted himself into a quantity and size and has acquired a physical identity, do not hesitate any longer to draw pictures and to set forth, for all to see, him who has chosen to let himself be seen: his ineffable descent from heaven to earth; his birth from the Virgin; his baptism in the Jordan; his transfiguration on Mount Tabor; the sufferings that have achieved for us freedom from suffering; the miracles that symbolized his divine nature and activity when they were performed through the activity of his [human] flesh; the burial, resurrection, and ascension into heaven by which the Savior has accomplished our salvation—describe all of these events, both in words and in colors, both in books and in pictures.

Thus the God who had prohibited religious art as the idolatrous effort to depict the

Contrary to a widespread impression, the ancient art of painting icons of Christ, of his Mother, and of his saints and apostles is not only an ancient art but a contemporary one, both in the historic territories of the Eastern Christian tradition and (as in an example from twentieth-century Canada) in New World communities where that tradition lives on.

divine in visible form had now taken the initiative of depicting himself in visible form, and had done so not in metaphor or in memorial but in person and, quite literally, "in the flesh." The metaphysical had become historical, and the cosmic Logos who was the true image of the Father from eternity had now become a part of time and could be portrayed in an image of his divine-human person as this had carried out the events of salvation history. The icons depicted the humanity of Jesus as suffused with the presence of divinity: it was, in this sense, the "deified" body of Christ that was being portrayed. The most characteristic Eastern Orthodox way of speaking about the salvation granted in Christ has been to call it "deification," by which, in the striking metaphors of the nineteenth-century poet and Jesuit priest Gerard Manley Hopkins, this "mortal trash," being made "what Christ is," became "immortal diamond." The iconography of the icon (to resort deliberately to a tautology) simultaneously depicted specificity and deification. By depicting the indissoluble union between the timeless nature of the All-Sovereign and the historical nature of Jesus of Nazareth, Byzantine icons of Christ portrayed the one who embodied not only the True in his teaching and the Good in his life but the Beautiful in his form as "the fairest of the sons of men" (Ps. 45:2).

Of that triad, the Beautiful took by far the longest time to evolve in Christian history. One of Augustine's early books, since lost, was called *On the Beautiful and the Fitting.* And in one of the most memorable passages of his *Confessions,* he exclaimed: "Too late have I loved Thee, Thou Beauty ever ancient ever new, too late have I come to love Thee!" As the iconoclasts saw with great clarity, the Beautiful is the most subtle and most seductive of the triad. The dangers of identifying the Holy with the True (intellectualism) and with the Good (moralism) have manifested themselves repeatedly in the history of Judaism and of Christianity, but it is noteworthy that the Bible singled out the identification of the Holy with the Beautiful as the special temptation to sin. The formulation of an aesthetic that came to terms with the reality of this temptation called for philosophical and theological sophistication. In addition, there had to have been an inspiration for religious art, an inspiration of more than a flatly didactic sort, before there could be any such aesthetic justification; and a sophisticated philosophical-theological challenge to religious art was necessary before any sophisticated defense of it was possible. All of this—inspiration, challenge, and justification—was eventually provided by the person of Jesus, who came to be seen as both the ground of continuity in art and the source of innovation for art, and thus, in a sense that Augustine could not have intended, as a "beauty ever ancient ever new."

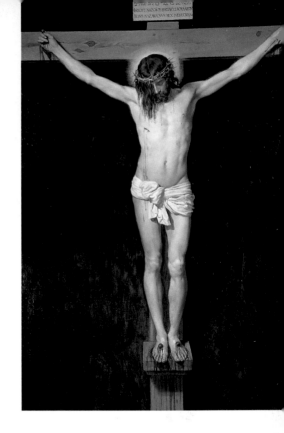

Therefore, friends,

As far as to the sepulchre of Christ,

Whose soldier now, under whose blessed cross

We are impressed and engaged to fight . . .

To chase those pagans in these holy fields

Over whose acres walk'd those blessed feet,

Which fourteen hundred years ago were nail'd

For our advantage on the bitter cross.

—*William Shakespeare,* I Henry IV

8 ✦ Christ Crucified

The followers of Jesus concluded very early that he had lived in order to die, that his death was not the interruption of his life but its ultimate purpose. The creeds recognized this by moving directly from his birth "from the Virgin Mary" to his crucifixion "under Pontius Pilate." What was said of the thane of Cawdor in *Macbeth* was true preeminently of Jesus: "Nothing in his life became him like the leaving it."

"Far be it from me," Paul said, "to glory except in the cross of our Lord Jesus Christ, by which the world has been crucified to me, and I to the world" (Gal. 6:14). But the gospel of the cross pervades the New Testament and early Christian literature. Christ was the "Lamb of God, who takes away the sin of the world" (John 1:29). The use of the sign of the cross appears early in Chris-

In both East and West the Christian view of Jesus Christ has been dominated by the belief that he lived in order to die. Nevertheless, Western Christendom has been the venue for the most brilliant speculation about that belief (by Anselm of Canterbury), the most detailed and graphic depictions of it (in art devoted to the crucifixion), and the most sublime musical celebration of it (in Bach's Saint Matthew Passion). *On the eve of the twentieth century, Edvard Munch's* Golgotha *depicted the centrality of death as transforming not only the appearance of the Crucified himself but that of the onlookers at the foot of the cross, whose faces seem at least as skeletal and spectral as his.*

tian history, and when it is mentioned it is already being taken for granted. Tertullian declares that "at every forward step and movement, at every going in and out . . . in all the ordinary actions of daily life, we mark upon our foreheads the sign." The sign of the cross of Jesus pervaded medieval culture—folklore, literature, music, art, and architecture—as no other symbol did. To lend coherence to these cruciform impressions, it may be useful to draw upon Paul's distinction: "Christ crucified. . . the power of God and the wisdom of God" (1 Cor. 1:23–24).

As the power of God, the sign of the cross was a talisman against evil. Medieval saints' lives are replete with stories of its wondrous powers. In one of the apocryphal *Acts* of the apostles, making the sign of the cross over a locked door causes it to open, and in one of the *Martyrdoms* the sign silences the barking of a dog. Augustine reports that a woman in Carthage, suffering from cancer of the breast, "was instructed in a dream to wait for the first woman who would come out of the baptistery after being baptized, and to ask her to make [the sign of the cross] upon her lesion. She did so and was cured immediately." Remaclus, a missionary, made the sign of the cross over a spring dedicated to pagan gods, driving out the gods and instantly purifying the water. An "ordeal of the cross" became, in medieval legal practice, a way of settling disputes; thus an eighth-century code prescribes: "If a woman claims that [her marriage has never been consummated], let them go out to the cross; and if it be true, let them be separated." We have reports of hemorrhages on the battlefield which no tourniquet could stanch but which the cross succeeded in stopping.

Sometimes it was even successful in raising the dead, and the crucifix had special power against vampires. There was a close connection between these uses of the cross and the belief in the power of demons. The sign of the cross could simultaneously serve as a magical amulet and, because of its inseparable association with the crucifixion of Jesus, act as a reminder that the power against demons and diseases was not resident in the amulet or the gesture but was in fact the power of God, who had come in the life and death of Jesus to break the power of evil.

A special case was the power in relics of the true cross, which in 326 Saint Helena was said to have found in a chamber under the present Church of the Holy Sepulcher in Jerusalem. Having done so, "the emperor's mother erected over the place of the sepulcher a magnificent church. . . . There she left a portion of the cross, enclosed in a silver case, as a memorial for those who might wish to see it. The other part she sent to the emperor, who, being persuaded that the city would be perfectly secure where that relic should be preserved, privately enclosed it in his own statue . . . at Constantinople." But these two were not to be the only portions. Less than a half-century later, Cyril of Jerusalem noted that "the whole world has been filled with pieces of the wood of the cross." We have references to such pieces of wood in Cappadocia and in Antioch during the second half of the fourth century, and by the beginning of the fifth century in Gaul; at the middle of that century the patriarch Juvenal of Jerusalem sent one to Pope Leo I in Rome. Pope Gregory I presented one to the queen of the Lombards, Theodelinde, and to Recared I, king of the

The identification of Christ as the "Lamb of God, who takes away the sin of the world" (John 1:29) received its most celebratory exposition in the Book of Revelation, where the Lamb who was slain has begun his reign and leads his followers in triumphant processions. In their gigantic altarpiece for the Church of Saint Bavo in Ghent, Hubert and Jan Van Eyck made that vision of the triumphant Lamb of God not only the center of the lower panel but the focus of the entire work.

Visigoths, who became a Catholic. Helena's discovery (or, as it was called in Latin and then with an unintentional irony in English, the "invention") of the cross was observed on 3 May (until it was abolished for the Latin rite during the Second Vatican Council). The true cross itself was captured by the Persians in the seventh century and recovered by the emperor Heraclius, but in the twelfth century it was carried into battle by the bishop of Bethlehem and lost—except, of course, for all those fragments.

The cross was believed to be "the power of God" above all in battle. After his victory at the Milvian Bridge, Constantine had ordered a banner of the cross to be carried into battle at the head of each of his armies. The "victory-granting cross" became a military insignia on land and sea, and in the West at the end of the eleventh century it became the central symbol of the Crusades to the Holy Land, as Shakespeare put it,

> over whose acres walk'd those blessed feet,
> Which fourteen hundred years ago were nail'd
> For our advantage on the bitter cross.

All this victorious power was ascribed to the cross because it had been the instrument for the greatest victory of them all, the cosmic victory of the power of God over the power of the devil in the death and resurrection of Jesus. "The word of the cross is called the power of God," John of Damascus said, "because the might of God, that is, his victory over death, has been revealed to us through it." The earliest versions of this idea had described the victory as a trick played on the unholy alliance of devil, death, and sin. In one of the most striking—and problematical—of images for the trick, the devil with his allies was depicted as a giant fish that had devoured every human being since Adam. When the humanity of Christ was cast into the pool, the fish took it as yet another victim. But hidden within this bait of the human nature of Christ was the hook of his divine nature, so that when the devil gobbled up the man Jesus in his death on the cross, he was impaled on the divinity. He had to regurgitate the humanity of Jesus, and with it all those whom Jesus had taken as his own; death and the devil, who had taken the human race, were now themselves taken. Through the cross came liberation and victory.

In a more subtle form, this theory of the cross became the metaphor of *Christus Victor*. Here the cross became the sign of God's invasion of enemy territory, the "wondrous battle" by which Jesus Christ accomplished salvation. Shedding the cruder metaphor of deception, the theme of Christus Victor retained the idea that on the cross Christ contended with the enemies of God and man. His death on the cross was his capitulation to their power, before which he made himself weak. Yet he took those enemies into the grave with him. In the resurrection Christ was freed from their power, but they remained behind in the grave. Although this interpretation of the cross as the power of God was more prominent in the Greek East than in the Latin West, it was never lost even in the West, and the Reformation revived it. In J. S. Bach's *Saint John Passion,* the dying words on the cross,

Although the story of the discovery of the True Cross by Saint Helena, mother of the emperor Constantine, originated in the East, in Constantinople and presumably in Jerusalem, it soon captured the imagination of Western believers and of Western poets and artists, finding its way into the popular collection The Golden Legend. *During the 1560s, Paolo Veronese's oil painting* The Vision of Saint Helena *caught the moment when, according to some versions of the story, two angels appeared to the empress carrying the cross, which she subsequently found.*

"It is finished!" become the occasion for an alto aria to exclaim:

> Lo, Judah's Lion wins with might
> And now victorious ends the fight:
> "It is finished!"

In the Middle Ages, Good Friday was the only day in the church year when the sacrifice of the Mass was not celebrated, because on that day worshipers commemorated the original sacrifice of the cross on Calvary. Medieval art depicted the crucifixion on the very place where the skull of Adam was buried, and processions and liturgical drama kept the motif of Christus Victor alive even when Latin theology could not deal with it adequately because of its preoccupation with the death of Christ as vicarious satisfaction.

An early poem in English, *The Dream of the Rood,* has the tree of the cross describe the "young Hero" who would ascend it for his combat with death and, succumbing in the combat, would nevertheless prevail. Venantius Fortunatus, "the first of the medieval poets," writing at the end of the sixth century, put the dramatic interpretation of the cross into two Latin poems that were to become a standard part of Lenten music. One of them, "Vexilla regis prodeunt," was the processional hymn for the fragment of the true cross sent to the Frankish queen by the Byzantine emperor:

> The royal banners forward go,
> The cross shines forth with mystic glow.

The other, "Pange, lingua," made Christus Victor even more explicit:

> Sing, my tongue, the glorious battle,
> Sing the ending of the fray.
> Now above the cross, the trophy,
> Sound the loud triumphant lay;
> Tell how Christ, the world's redeemer,
> As a victim won the day.

Another ancient literary device adapted to the sign of the cross was the figured poem, which combined poetic and visual forms by varying the length of the lines in a prescribed shape. In *The Praises of the Holy Cross* by the ninth-century theologian Rabanus Maurus, the dominant theme was Christus Victor. Most of its verses are cast in the form of square grids formed by a number of letters equal to the number of lines in the text of that verse, which permitted crosses with arms of equal length to be superimposed on the text. A further elaboration was to arrange the symbols for the evangelists—a man (Matthew), a lion (Mark), an ox (Luke), and an eagle (John)—in the form of a cross.

As the symbol of God's power, the cross was also the sign of God's wisdom, which, as "the foolishness of God," was wiser than any vaunted human wisdom (1 Cor. 1:25). "As the

wisdom of the world is foolishness to God," Tertullian said, "so also the wisdom of God is foolishness in the world's esteem." In seeking to celebrate the cross as wisdom, writers and artists often took pains to revel first in its "foolishness," as in the paradox of Augustine's statement: "The deformity of Christ forms you. If he had not willed to be deformed, you would not have recovered the form you had lost. Therefore he was deformed when he hung on the cross. But his deformity is our comeliness. In this life, therefore, let us hold fast to the deformed Christ." Above all, the mystery of the cry of dereliction on the cross, "My God, my God, why hast thou forsaken me?" evoked awe and consternation. The beginning of wisdom was the acceptance of that mystery: the one whom Christians believed to be "one in being with the Father" had been—whatever sense anyone could make of it all—forsaken by his Father on the cross.

When they spoke of the cross as wisdom, it was often to cite Jesus on the cross as an example of patience and charity even in the midst of suffering: "For to this you have been called, because Christ also suffered for you, leaving you an example, that you should follow in his steps. He committed no sin; no guile was found on his lips. When he was reviled, he did not revile in return; when he suffered, he did not threaten; but he trusted to him who judges justly" (1 Pet. 2:21–23). One of the most widely read books in the Middle Ages was the late-sixth-century *Moralia* of Pope Gregory I, a massive exposition of the Book of Job, which considered the sufferings of that pre-Christian saint so as to direct at-

The hymn "Vexilla regis prodeunt [The royal banners forward go]" by the Christian Latin poet Venantius Fortunatus celebrated a festival procession in which a relic of the true cross, the gift of the Byzantine emperor to the Franks and their princess, was borne before a large crowd of worshipers. Many centuries later, in 1496, Gentile Bellini memorialized a similar procession held in 1444, as the relic of the true cross owned by the School of Saint John the Evangelist was borne through the piazza before the Basilica of Saint Mark in Venice.

Because the New Testament (Rom. 5, 1 Cor. 15) characterized Jesus Christ as the Second Adam, who came to repair the damage wrought by the First Adam, Christian imagination sought parallels between the two: the temptation in Genesis 3 and the temptation in Matthew 4; the Garden of Eden and the Garden of Gethsemane; the tree of the knowledge of good and evil and the tree of the cross. A particularly imaginative instance of such parallelism was the belief, which developed without explicit biblical warrant, that the cross of Christ was planted on Mount Golgotha at the very spot where the skull of Adam was buried, "that whence death arose, thence also life might rise again." From opposite corners of Western Europe come two versions of that belief, once again from Saint Mark's in Venice and from Albrecht Dürer's Great Passion *of 1498.*

tention through them to the exemplary sufferings of Jesus. Three centuries later, in Odo's epic about Paradise lost and regained, Christ, who came to save the world from pride, "teaches this especially by all the things that he does in utmost humility, saying, 'I am meek, all of you learn this from me' (Matt. 11:29)."

But the imitation of Christ's example was never the whole of the meaning of the cross. Its very shape was said to have justified the ways of God to man, the vertical and the horizontal bars representing the height and the breadth of the universe, and their point of convergence where the head of Christ was laid representing the unification and ultimate harmony of all in Christ crucified. For the cross was the most evident of all proofs for the power of evil in the world; Jesus said to his captors (Luke 22:53), "This is your hour, and the power of darkness." But it was at the same time the supreme proof that the will and way of God would eventually prevail, regardless of what human plans might conspire to do. True wisdom, the wisdom of the cross, consisted in the ability to hold these together, neither ignoring the presence and power of evil, as a superficial optimism was tempted to do, nor allowing the presence and power of evil to negate the sovereignty of the one God,

To explain the unexplainable mystery of redemption through Christ, one persistent theory has been that his death on the cross atoned for the sins of the human race by rendering satisfaction to the violated justice (or "rectitude") of God, thus establishing the conditions for the mercy of God to grant forgiveness. As expounded in a treatise of 1098, Why God Became Man *by Anselm, the Benedictine monk and archbishop of Canterbury for whom Sant' Anselmo in Rome is named, the theory continued to claim the authority of the sixteenth-century Reformers and of much of Protestantism ever since.*

as a fatalistic dualism tended to do. Thus the providence of God, which Boethius defined in relation to fate as "the divine type itself, seated in the Supreme Ruler, which disposes all things," became, in the hands of Thomas Aquinas, a part of his examination of the activity of God in relation to the world, an examination whose ultimate foundation was the unmerited love of God.

The wisdom of the cross was, then, the disclosure not only of human morality but of divine love. The medieval French theologian Peter Abelard, in an essay entitled "The Cross," emphasized that the love of God in Christ lay beyond "our own power to share in the passion of Jesus by our suffering and to follow him by carrying our own cross." The fundamental meaning of the wisdom of the cross was contained in the words of Jesus: "Greater love has no man than this, that a man lay down his life for his friends" (John 15:13). The purpose of the cross was to thaw the frozen hearts of sinners with the warmth of divine love. Christ died on the cross not to change the mind of God (which, like everything about God, was unchangeable) but "to reveal the love [of God] to us or to convince us how much we ought to love him 'who did not spare even his own Son' (Rom. 8:32) for us." This exhibited the authentic nature of love and the depth of divine love, thus making human love, even self-sacrificing human love, possible.

Abelard's critics found such language about the wisdom of the cross inadequate. The question was whether a more profound consideration of the cross would lead to some other way of thinking and speaking about it. That other way found its definitive formulation in the treatise *Why God Became Man* by Anselm of Canterbury, often called the founder of scholasticism. Anselm develops his argument, as he says, "as though Christ did not exist," proceeding by reason alone. The underlying presupposition was the consistency of God and the universe, which God did not violate by arbitrary acts that would undermine the moral order of the universe, its "rightness [*rectitudo*]." Rightness consisted in rendering to each a due measure of honor. Although created for participation in rightness, the human race refused to give God due honor and fell into sin. This was something that God could not simply overlook or forgive by fiat without violating "rightness"; such was the demand of divine justice. Yet both human wisdom and divine revelation made it clear that God was a God not only of justice but of mercy, who declared: "I have no pleasure in the death of the wicked, but that the wicked turn from his way and live" (Ezek. 33:11).

Such was the divine dilemma resolved by the wisdom of the cross. For the justice of God, having pronounced that violation of the moral order was worthy of death, clashed with the mercy of God, which desired life rather than death. The one who was guilty of the sin, man, could not pay the penalty except by being lost forever; the one who wanted to forgive, God, could not do so except by undercutting the moral order of the universe. Only a being able to pay the penalty (by being human) but capable of making a payment that was of infinite worth (by being divine) could simultaneously carry out the imperatives of divine mercy and satisfy the demands of divine justice. The payment, moreover, had to be voluntary and could not be made by someone who owed it on his own behalf, for that would not avail for others. Therefore God had to become a man and die on the cross, so as to achieve the ends of divine mercy and yet render satisfaction to divine justice and thus uphold "rightness." His death on the cross made it, one may say, morally possible for God to forgive.

Anselm's doctrine of satisfaction embodied themes from the penitential practice and canon law of the church: a sinner who was truly contrite and confessed his sin was absolved but had to make restitution of what the sin had taken away. So it was on a cosmic scale with the sin of the entire human race, and the death of Christ on the cross was such an act of restitution and reparation, to which human acts of satisfaction then attached themselves. Anselm set forth a "wisdom of the cross" that was to be perceived by human reason as well as through divine revelation.

At every level of its culture, medieval society, whether Eastern or Western, was pervaded by the sign of the cross, both literally and figuratively. Thus, regardless of the historical credence anyone may be prepared to give the statement of Cyril of Jerusalem quoted earlier, that "the whole world has been filled with pieces of the wood of the cross," we may see in the Middle Ages the fulfillment of another statement, apparently more modest but actually more extravagant, in the first paragraph of the first book written by Cyril's older contemporary, Athanasius of Alexandria: "The power of the cross of Christ has filled the world."

Jesus, I my cross have taken,
All to leave and follow Thee.
Destitute, despised, forsaken,
Thou from hence my All shalt be.
—*Henry Francis Lyte*
  Poems Chiefly Religious

9 ❖ The Monk Who Rules the World

The words of Jesus that underlie this epigraph (Matt. 16:24) have always been a summons to self-denial for all his disciples. But early in the sixth century they became the charter of Western Christian monasticism, which denied the world for the sake of Christ—and then went on to conquer the world in the name of Christ, the Monk who ruled the world. Although Jesus' way of life contrasted with that of the more ascetic John the Baptist (Luke 7:31–35), the fundamental imperatives of the monastic life were no less fundamental to the portrait of Jesus in all four Gospels. The monks began by patterning themselves after Christ; they likewise patterned Christ after themselves. The motif of "Christ the Monk" is carried out in monastic manuscripts and altarpieces of the Middle Ages as well as in modern adaptations.

The Life of Antony, *inspired by the Egyptian founder of Christian asceticism and written in Greek by Athanasius in the middle fourth century, was almost immediately translated into Latin. Therefore it could be read also in the West, for example by Augustine. It was supplemented by other Western writers, including Jerome, who composed* The Life of Saint Paul the Hermit. *Thus the "old man who had lived the life of a hermit" whom Athanasius describes as having been visited by Antony came to be identified with Paul the Hermit; the satyr stands for the pagan hedonism over which Christ was seen as having triumphed through their asceticism.*

Christian monasticism is, in a sense, older than Christianity, for there already were hermits and monastic communities, Jewish as well as pagan. In the Egyptian desert dwelt the Jewish Therapeutae, described by Philo of Alexandria, a contemporary of Jesus, in *On the Contemplative Life*. Christian asceticism in Egypt found its most abiding expression in Saint Antony, and in the influential *Life of Antony* prepared after his death by Athanasius. One of its Western readers was Augustine, who established a monastic community and wrote for it a letter that became the basis of the *Rule of St. Augustine*. Yet by far the most influential document of Western asceticism and one of the most influential documents of Western civilization is the *Rule of Benedict* a century later. It was the central purpose of Benedict's *Rule* to teach novice monks how to "renounce themselves in order to follow Christ," how to "advance in the ways [of Christ] with the Gospel as our guide," and, by persevering in the monastic life, how to "share by patience in the passion of Christ and hereafter deserve to be united with him in his kingdom"—in a single formula, "not to value anything more highly than the love of Christ." The love of Christ, moreover, modified one of the basic impulses that led to monasticism. "Deep in the monastic consciousness is solitude," writes a historian of asceticism. But, he continues, "you discover to your vexation that deep in the Christian consciousness ran the axiom that you must receive strangers as though they were Christ, and they really might be Christ." Therefore, quoting the Gospel (Matt. 25:35), Benedict specified in his *Rule:* "All guests coming to the monastery shall be received as Christ." Benedict was defining the life of the monk as a participation in the life of Christ. All three virtues vowed by the monk—poverty, chastity, and obedience—were based on Christ as pattern and embodiment.

Although the ascetic impulse, as articulated by Paul (1 Cor. 7:1–7), had been present in the Christian movement from the beginning, it is no coincidence that it rose to prominence as the church was making its peace with the Roman empire and the world. Part of the price for that peace was coming to terms with those who were willing to go along with being Christians much as they had been willing to go along with being pagans, just as long as it did not cost them too much. Now that it was easier to be a nominal Christian than to be a nominal pagan, the multitudes who began to crowd into the church were not looking to become "athletes" for Christ; but that was precisely the term Athanasius used to describe Antony the ascetic, with his rigorous training to compete and win in Christ's contest against the devil, the world, and the flesh. These monastic athletes, as one scholar has put it, "were not only fleeing from the world in every sense of the word, they were fleeing from the worldly church." The monasticism of the fourth and fifth centuries was a protest, in the name of the authentic teaching of Jesus, against an almost inevitable by-product of the Constantinian settlement, the secularization of the church.

This introduced into the life and teaching of the church a double standard of discipleship, dividing the demands of Jesus into "commandments," which implied "necessity" and

The original monastery of Monte Cassino was built by Benedict about 529, becoming the mother house for Benedictine monasteries all over the world and derivatively for all other Western monasteries and convents as well. Repeatedly it has been destroyed in war: by the Lombards about 585, by the Muslims in 884, by the Normans in 1046, and by the Allied bombers in 1944 (with the thoroughness visible in the first photograph). Repeatedly it has also been restored, as in 1950–54 (with the stateliness visible in the second photograph).

were taken as binding on everyone, and "counsels of perfection," which were "left to choice" and were binding only on monastic athletes. "If you would be perfect," Jesus had said, "go, sell what you possess and give to the poor"; at the same time he had spoken of those "who have made themselves eunuchs for the sake of the kingdom of heaven" (Matt. 19:21, 12). These were not commandments setting down what was necessary for salvation but counsels of perfection; to make that clear, Jesus had appended the proviso: "He who is able to receive this, let him receive it." The medieval church defined matrimony as a sacrament but never made either celibacy or monastic vows a sacrament—although ordination to the priesthood, which in the West came to presuppose celibacy, was one of the seven sacraments. Nevertheless, the Sermon on the Mount demanded "perfection" of its hearers (Matt. 5:48); the meaning of perfection was increasingly sought not in the family life and daily work of the Christian believer within society but in the life of the monk and the nun, to whom the word *religious* was applied as a technical term.

Yet this protest against a secularized church became a means of conquering the church and the world. The most striking mark of this monastic conquest in the Byzantine church was the requirement of celibacy for the bishop. The East consistently opposed the efforts of the West to make celibacy a requirement for all parish clergy, but the legislation of the Eastern provinces of the church eventually specified that although parish clergy could remain married, bishops had to be celibate. This combination of rules granted monks a virtual monopoly on the episcopate. As a fifteenth-century Greek archbishop was to put it, monasticism "is endowed with such prestige and standing that practically the entire church seems to be governed by monks. Thus if you make diligent inquiry, you will hardly find anyone who has been promoted to the sacred hierarchy from the world [including the secular clergy]; for this has been allotted to the monks. And you know that if some are appointed to the holy offices [of bishop or patriarch], it is stipulated by the church that they should first put on the monastic habit." When—as in the notorious case of the scholar Photius, selected as patriarch of Constantinople in 858—the choice fell on a layman, the result was that "the monastic world all but unanimously refused allegiance to the new patriarch." During the conflicts over the icons in the century preceding Photius's election, Byzantine monks had played a decisive role stirring up the populace in support of images. After the iconoclastic controversies it became a rule for the patriarch-elect or bishop-elect to be a monk, or to become one. Those who had fled from the world that was in the church acquired dominion over the church that was in the world.

The dominant position of the monk in Eastern Orthodoxy made itself visible in the works of the two best-known literary descendants of Eastern Orthodoxy in the nineteenth century, Fyodor Dostoyevsky and Leo Tolstoy. Father Zossima in *The Brothers Karamazov* is the embodiment and advocate of the monastic ideal: "How surprised men would be if I were to say that from these meek monks, who yearn for solitary prayer, the

When the Rule of Benedict *is compared with its predecessors (notably the so-called* Rule of the Master*) and with its successors, the impressive quality that emerges from it is its blending of strictness and humaneness, evangelical fervor and practical wisdom. It is not surprising that those who lived by the* Rule *attributed it to angelic inspiration, as did the unknown tenth-century painter of this miniature preserved in the library of Benedict's monastery, Monte Cassino.*

salvation of Russia will perhaps come once more! For they are in truth made ready in peace and quiet for the day and the hour, the month and the year. Meanwhile, in their solitude, they keep the image of Christ fair and undefiled, in the purity of God's truth, from the times of the fathers of old, the apostles and the martyrs." Tolstoy, meanwhile, who radically rejected Russian Orthodoxy, nevertheless emerges as the "authentic Greek monk."

In the Latin West, the career of Jesus the Monk in the development of monasticism throughout the Middle Ages is the history of successive reform movements. Each was intent on bringing rejuvenation to the monastic ideal; on achieving, through such a rejuvenation of the monastic ideal, the renewal of the church and the papacy; and on redeeming

and purifying medieval society through such a renewal of church and papacy. The intellectual and institutional evolution of these reform movements during the thousand years between Benedict of Nursia (who founded the monastery of Monte Cassino in about 529) and Martin Luther (who entered the monastery of the Augustinian Hermits at Erfurt in 1505) is a story of inestimable historical importance. There is a depressing repetition of pattern, as each reform in its turn protests against decline and stagnation in the monasteries, sets up new administrative and disciplinary structures to reverse the downward trend, prevails for a century or two, and then proves itself vulnerable to the same tendencies. In each instance, however, it bears noting that reform was once again possible, as the transforming power of the figure of Jesus the Monk reasserted itself and as Jesus returned yet once more "and drove out all who sold and bought in the temple" (Matt. 21:12)—at least temporarily.

Eastern Christian monasticism does not have a "mother house" corresponding to Monte Cassino. Instead, it has the cluster of some twenty autonomous monastic houses of "the Holy Mountain," Mount Athos on the Aegean Sea, as shown on the map on page 125. They have varied in number and in quality over the centuries, but each has maintained its ties to the mother church in its home country. The Monastery of Dionysiou is shown here.

In both the Eastern and the Western traditions, the person of Jesus Christ stands at the center of monastic life for the individual and for the entire community. What the Rule of Benedict *prescribes for Roman Catholic monks, "not to value anything more highly than the love of Christ," is what Eastern Orthodox monks teach and practice as well, as they gather for meals under the dominating gaze of Christ in this fresco from the refectory of the Monastery of Dionysiou, Mount Athos.*

The observation that in the East "practically the entire church seems to be governed by monks" meant that the monasteries have provided leadership not only in the missionary enterprise, as they have also in the West, but in the life and administration of the churches, where they have become the bishops. Saint Sava (depicted on page 125), a member of the Serbian royal family, who was living as a monk on Mount Athos, returned to Serbia in 1208 and obtained for it an "auto-cephalous," or independently administered, Orthodox church.

Through these reform movements, the monastic conquest of the church sought to make itself ever more complete. Early in the fourth century, regional synods in Spain required celibacy of parish clergy, and by the end of that century a series of popes and councils made this universal. Only several centuries later, however, could the requirement be enforced. That enforcement is associated with the work of Hildebrand, the eleventh-century reformer who was the gray eminence of the papacy for a quarter-century before finally becoming pope in his own right in 1073 as Gregory VII. His training under the influence of the Cluniac order, with its dedication to rooting out the corruptions that infected Benedictine monasticism, convinced him that the way to conform church and papacy to the will of Christ was by restoring monastic life to its original ideals and then applying those ideals to the life of the church as a whole. A basic component of that reform was the enforcement of clerical celibacy, which may be defined, in a formula adopted by Pope John Paul II, as an imitation of Jesus Christ by which "a priest is a man who lives alone so that others should not be alone." In the setting of the eleventh century, celibacy was a way to secure the independence of the priest and bishop from secular authorities. Yet Pope Gregory VII saw in this administrative reform nothing less than a spiritual renewal of the church's dedication to Christ.

That new dedication became a means for the reconquest of the world for Christ. In the Gospel of Matthew the charter of Christian monasticism (Matt. 16:24) appears just a few verses after the charter of the papacy, the words of Jesus to Peter: "I tell you, you are Peter [*Petros*], and on this rock [*petra*] I will build my church, and the powers of death shall not prevail against it. I will give you the keys of the kingdom of heaven, and whatever you bind on earth shall be bound in heaven, and whatever you loose on earth shall be loosed in heaven" (Matt. 16:18–19). Quoting those words, Gregory VII set the terms for Christ's reconquest of the world and of the empire: "Now then tell me, are kings an exception to this rule? Do they not also belong to the sheep which the Son of God has entrusted to the blessed Peter? Who, I ask, can regard himself as excluded from the power of Peter in this universal grant of authority to forbid and to allow, except perhaps for someone who declines to bear the yoke of the Lord [Jesus], who subjects himself instead to the burden of the devil, and who refuses to be counted among the sheep of Christ?" In the confrontation with Emperor Henry IV at Canossa in 1077, Gregory VII, having been addressed by the emperor as "Hildebrand, at present not pope but false monk," reaffirmed the authority of Christ to bind and loose sins by granting absolution to Henry. Hildebrand the monk had apparently conquered not only the church and the papacy but the empire and the world, in the name of Jesus the Monk.

Another such conquest was to come just over half a century later, when a Cistercian abbot and disciple of Bernard of Clairvaux was elected pope as Eugenius III in 1145. To his son in Christ who was now his father in Christ, Bernard addressed the treatise *On Consideration*. He admonished his former pupil not to allow the administrative details of the papacy to deflect him from what was primary in the church: the person of Jesus Christ. The pope should become the successor of Peter, not of Constantine. For the monastic ideals of contemplation and study were not irrelevant to the governance of the church but central to it. The subsequent use of Bernard's treatise by church reformers of every stripe in the fifteenth and sixteenth centuries is a documentation of how the monastic ideal of denying the world for Christ did indeed conquer the world for Christ.

One of the most lasting of monastic conquests for Christ was the work of medieval missions. The Christianization of the tribes who came into Europe, it has been said, "was brought about by the continual self-sacrifice and heroic labors of hundreds of monks in all parts of Europe." Protestant scholars like the leading historian of missions, Kenneth Scott Latourette, have likewise acknowledged that the name of Jesus Christ would have remained largely unknown in Europe and in the Americas "but for the monks." Thus the apostles to the Slavs, Cyril and Methodius, were Byzantine monks; and by designating them as "joint patron saints of Europe" together with Benedict, Pope John Paul II has once again recognized the decisive contribution of Western and Eastern monks to the mission and expansion of Christianity. Conversely, the abolition of the monastic orders

Few monks have left such an impress on their own and subsequent times as Bernard of Clairvaux (d. 1153). He was one of the great preachers of history, as is evident even now from his Sermons on the Song of Songs. *Bernard was the leading medieval devotee of the Virgin Mary, who visited him in visions and who is the subject of the praises he indites at the close of Dante's* Divine Comedy. *And when a disciple of his was elected pope as Eugenius III in 1145, Bernard addressed to him the treatise* On Consideration, *which became a standard manual of church reform.*

From the Benedictine Abbey of Saint John the Baptist in Collegeville, Minnesota, comes a twentieth-century statue of Pax Christi, *"the Peace of Christ," which shows him in Benedictine garb, holding the book of the Gospel in his left hand and pronouncing the Pax, or benediction, with his right. At the same time he is pronouncing the summons to all (and not only to monks) that they deny the world, take up the cross, and follow him.*

by the sixteenth-century Reformers was a major reason for the loss of the missionary imperative in most of Protestantism for more than two centuries.

There is no indication that Benedict envisaged a missionary role for his monks when he founded Monte Cassino. There is likewise nothing in the *Rule* that would have led inevitably to another of the great conquests of Benedictine monasticism, its dominance of European scholarship; for "no judgment either favorable or unfavorable as to the worth of learning or of the study of letters is to be found in the *Rule* of St. Benedict." One way to

Jesu, Lover of my soul,
Let me to Thy bosom fly,
While the nearer waters roll,
While the tempest still is high.
—Charles Wesley
 In Temptation

10❖The Bridegroom of the Soul

Charles Wesley seems to have written these familiar words soon after the conversion of his brother John in 1738. Since then, as the *Dictionary of Hymnology* says, "its popularity increases with its age, and few collections are now found from which it is excluded." Nevertheless, as the *Dictionary* also notes, "the opening stanza of this hymn has given rise to questions which have resulted in more than twenty different readings of the first four lines. The first difficulty is the term *Lover* as applied to our Lord," which various revisions have bowdlerized to "Refuge" or "Savior." A few years earlier, Count Nikolaus von Zinzendorf, founder of the Herrnhut Moravian Church, had written the no less popular hymn "Seelenbräutigam, O du Gottes Lamm!" (Bridegroom of the soul, thou Lamb of God!).

Such titles for Jesus belong to the realm of discourse usually labeled "Christ-mysticism." If mysticism may be defined as "the immediate experience of oneness with Ultimate Reality," Christ-mysticism is what emerged when the figure of Jesus of Nazareth became the object of mystical experience, thought, and language. Standing in the succession of the prophets, the message of Jesus has sometimes been interpreted as the very antithesis of the mystical; for, in the epigrammatic distinction of Abraham Heschel, a twentieth-century Jewish theologian, "What is important in mystical acts is that *something happens,* what is important in prophetic acts is that *something is said.*" And yet the prophetic literature of the Hebrew Bible is replete with what sounds very much like mystical experience, thought, and language. In postbiblical Judaism, moreover, these elements have frequently assumed a dominant role.

The rise of Christ-mysticism was most closely associated not with this tradition but with the de-Judaization of Christianity. Much of the vocabulary of mysticism—the understanding of the way to a relation with Ultimate Reality as an ascent, as well as the classic enumeration of the three steps of that mystical ascent as purification, illumination, and union—came from Neoplatonic sources. Therefore it did not come as a shock when, in the sixth century, there appeared a blend of Christian and Neoplatonic elements allegedly written by Dionysius the Areopagite, the only man named as having "believed" at Athens when Paul preached there (Acts 17:34) and, according to tradition, the first bishop of Athens. Certified as it was with such impressive and all-but-apostolic credentials, this body of writings by "Dionysius" was accepted as authentic almost without dissent for an entire millennium, not being seriously challenged until the fifteenth and sixteenth centuries. What place does the person of Jesus occupy in this mystical schema? The answer is not easy. For although, in the words of one prominent Orthodox historian, John Meyendorff, "undoubtedly Dionysius . . . mentions the name of Jesus Christ and professes his belief in the incarnation," it must be acknowledged that "the structure of his system is perfectly independent of his profession of faith. 'Jesus' is for him . . . 'the principle, the essence . . . of all holiness and of all divine operation,'" but not in any central or decisive sense the son of Mary and the man of Nazareth. The subsequent history of the Christ-mysticism inspired by this source manifests a complex synthesis of Neoplatonic and biblical elements.

A major inspiration of Christ-mysticism was the Song of Songs. Originally a poem celebrating the love between man and woman, the Song has throughout its history been read allegorically, and it may even have come into the Jewish canon that way. The best-known allegorical exposition of the Song is probably that of Bernard of Clairvaux, but as Bernard's biographer and editor, Jean Leclercq, has noted, it was "the book which was most read, and most frequently commented [upon] in the medieval cloister," more even than the four Gospels. And while, to use Leclercq's distinction, a scholastic commentary on the book "speaks mostly of God's relations with the entire Church, . . . the monastic

From the single reference
in the Book of Acts to Dionysius
the Areopagite as the only man
who "believed" when Paul preached
at Athens (Acts 17:34), the tradition
arose that he was the first bishop
of Athens. Then a collection of
writings bearing his name appeared
in the sixth century, blending
Christian and Neoplatonic
elements. He was celebrated
in this seventeenth-century
Greek icon by Emmanuel
Tzanes.

commentary's object is rather God's relations with each soul, Christ's presence in it, the spiritual union realized through charity." In eighty-six sermons Bernard covered the first two chapters and the beginning of the third, transforming the Song into an account of Jesus as the Bridegroom of the Soul. "By inspiration from above [Solomon] sang the praises of Christ and his church, the grace of holy love, and the sacraments of eternal marriage; and at the same time he gave expression to the deepest desires of the holy soul." The "kiss" of which the Song speaks is Jesus: "He it is whose speech, living and powerful, is to me a kiss . . . the imparting of joys, the revelation of secrets." The soul responds to the summons of its Bridegroom and follows him into the chamber of his love. As an earlier commentary on this verse had put it, "This done, the two are united: God comes to the soul, and the soul in turn unites itself with God. For she says, 'My beloved is mine and I am his, he pastures his flock among the lilies.' [I am] his who has transformed our human nature from the realm of shadowy appearances to that of ultimate truth."

The mystical concept of "ascent" provided the framework for one of the masterpieces of medieval Christ-mysticism, *The Soul's Journey into God* by Bonaventure. The mind begins among the visible creatures of the sensible world, but it is filled with awe and aspires to rise higher. Its contemplation of itself, because of "the mirror of our mind," fills it with a longing for increased and higher experience of God. By successive stages, then, the mind

The very ambiguity of the word "passion," in Latin as in English, enabled the piety of Bernard of Clairvaux to translate and sublimate the language of the Song of Solomon about the love between man and woman into a celebration of the love manifested by Christ in his passion and death. Jeronimo Jacinto de Espinosa's Saint Bernard of Clairvaux Carrying the Instruments of the Passion *makes that sublimated language visible.*

moves from creature to Creator. To do this, the mystic must acknowledge the primacy of will and of love. For each stage of the mystical ascent, according to Bonaventure, the "ladder" of the human nature of Jesus is decisive, as we rise from his feet to the wounds in his side to his head. In this way the three stages of mystical ascent were easily adaptable to this imagery of Christ as Bridegroom of the Soul. Before the soul can dare to hope for the object of its longing, it must be purged of impurity and receive the forgiveness of sins. But it

must be purified as well of its preoccupation with carnal things. Because of the inborn carnality of all human beings, "God the Word became flesh"—incarnate and in that sense "carnal." Only thus could he "draw to the saving love of his sacred flesh all the affections of carnal men who were unable to love otherwise than in a carnal manner, and so by degrees to draw them to a pure and spiritual affection." Jesus moved from infancy through to manhood in order to grant this purification to every age of human life.

The second step of the mystical ascent was illumination. This is well exemplified in the words of the fourteenth-century visionary Julian of Norwich, who has been called "in qualities of mind and heart, one of the most remarkable—perhaps the most remarkable—Englishwoman of her age." For Julian, "the light is God, our Maker, Father, and Holy Ghost in Christ Jesus our Saviour." The suffering and cross of Jesus become a way of

The general of the Franciscan Order, Bonaventure (d. 1274), represented on an altarpiece by the "Master of the Glorification of Mary" in Cologne (opposite page), devoted his short book The Soul's Journey into God *to the stages by which, climbing up the "ladder" of the human nature of Jesus, from his feet to the wounds in his side to his head, the "ascent" of the soul could bring it into the presence of God.*

Many visions of Christ were granted to mystical women in the Middle Ages, for example to Julian of Norwich, whom a leading historian of Christian mysticism has called "in qualities of mind and heart, one of the most remarkable— perhaps the most remarkable— Englishwoman of her age." In the mystical vision of light, according to Julian, "the light is God, our Maker, Father, and Holy Ghost in Christ Jesus our Saviour."

overcoming what she calls the "darkness of sin" and the "blindness" of the soul. For, she says, the darkness of sin "hath no manner of substance nor particle of being" and is not a reality in its own right but the absence of light. Only with the coming of the light that is Jesus and with the revelation of his suffering, does the power of this unreal darkness become evident and thereby lose its hold. As another English mystic, the seventeenth-century poet and cleric Robert Herrick, put it,

> And these mine eyes shall see
> All times, how they
> Are lost i' th' Sea
> Of vast Eternìtie.

A miniature from the Rothschild Canticles *quotes and illustrates the words from the opening of the final book of Augustine's* Confessions: *"I call you into my soul, which you are preparing for your reception, through the longing which you have inspired in it." This is the longing of the soul for its Bridegroom, who descends to it from the heavens and to whom it responds in ecstasy, an ecstasy that the Bridegroom himself has "inspired in it."*

After purification and illumination will come union. Here it was especially the language of the Gospel of John that lent itself to the uses of Christ-mysticism. "Abide in me, and I in you," Jesus says to the disciples (John 15:4); and in his high-priestly prayer on the night of his betrayal he implores his Father for his followers, "that they may all be one; even as thou, Father, art in me, and I in thee, that they also may be in us" (John 17:21). When such sayings of Jesus were combined with the words of the Song of Songs, "My Beloved is mine and I am his," the eternal union between Jesus and the Father in the mystery of the holy and indivisible Trinity became the ground for "the mystical union" between bride and Bridegroom, Christ and the soul.

Dante's *Divine Comedy* may be read as a celebration of these three stages—not as though *Inferno, Purgatorio,* and *Paradiso* corresponded to purification, illumination, and union, for none of the three is possible in hell; but the three themes mark the steps of the soul's ascent, and thus of the poet's ascent. The *Purgatorio*'s recitation of the means by which each of the seven mortal sins is purged away through penance and the grace of

Christ is an almost clinical analysis of what the mystics meant by the "way of purgation." The illumination sought by Christ-mysticism is proclaimed in the opening lines of the *Paradiso:* "The glory of Him who moves all things penetrates the universe and shines in one part more and another less. I was in the heaven that most receives His light." And in the closing canto of the *Paradiso,* Dante turns, as mystics like Bonaventure had said one must, to the will and to its desire, which bring him to harmony and union with divine Love.

The themes of purification, illumination, and mystical union with Christ the Bridegroom of the Soul also shaped the depictions of the lives of the saints in both literature and art. The thirteenth-century Franciscan saint Margaret of Cortona, "the new Magdalene," is an especially striking example, for her revelations and mystical experiences resulted from a conversion to Christ that followed the tragic death of a young nobleman with whom she had been living for nine years outside the sacrament of matrimony. The *Acts of the Saints* tells us that "she heard Jesus Christ calling her in a sweet manner" and that, "lifted up to the extremes of ecstasy, she lost all consciousness and motion." Medieval mystics and thinkers sought to curb the potential dangers of this language. The Song remains an explicit love poem, and the allegory can easily revert to the very eroticism it is intended to transcend. In many poems of the medieval troubadours, as their editor Thomas Bergin has put it, "the worship of the lady suggests a kind of literary mariolatry; but the love celebrated, for all its refinement, was adulterous." Lyrics addressed to the Blessed Virgin Mary and lyrics addressed to a sweetheart often became interchangeable, with the devotional lines being used to conceal—and thus to reveal—the poet's true desire for his lady love. The word *soul* is feminine in most of the languages of Europe, making it all the easier to transpose the metaphors about the Bridegroom of the Soul into highly charged sexual images. The line from emotion to sentimentality was easy to cross, and so was the line from holy love for Christ to erotic love for Christ; it was just as easy to cross both lines at once.

Also easy to cross, especially in the later Middle Ages, was the line separating Christ-mysticism from pantheism. The yearning for union with the divine frequently seemed to become a yearning for the obliteration of the distinction between Creator and creature. Jewish mysticism had frequently addressed this problem, but for Christ-mysticism the temptation appears to have been even more insidious. Various mystics of the fifteenth century were accused of harboring an eschatology in which everything, having come from God, would be reabsorbed into God.

Likewise implicit in many strains of Christ-mysticism, already in the Middle Ages and even more in later Protestantism, was individualism; in the words of one extreme critic, "In the midst of its struggle for unselfish love, mysticism proves to be the most refined form, the acme of egocentric piety." "My beloved is mine and I am his" became a way of describing a person's private relation to Jesus, and Jesus' relation to that person, to the ex-

*Margaret of Cortona,
positioned by Guercino in
an act of adoration before the
Crucified, was converted from a
life of sensuality with an illicit lover,
which she had mistakenly equated
with love,* to a life of genuine love
for the Bridegroom of the Soul; *for
according to the* Acts of the Saints,
*"she heard Jesus Christ calling her
in a sweet manner," and, "lifted up
to the extremes of ecstasy, she
lost all consciousness
and motion."*

clusion, or at least the diminution, of others. A well-known sentimental religious song has expressed this individualism quite unabashedly:

> And He walks with me and He talks with me,
> And He tells me I am His own.
> And the joys we share, as we tarry there,
> *None other has ever known.*

Responding to the deepest yearnings of the human spirit for transcendent meaning and authentic fulfillment, the experience of purification, illumination, and union with the "Beautiful Savior" has ennobled every natural sensibility and elevated it into a means of grace: nothing need be profane, everything can be sacramental. Yet it carried the real danger of dissolving the history of Jesus Christ into a generalized spirituality. Cutting itself loose as it does from the strict grammatical sense of the biblical text, a mystical exegesis is especially vulnerable on this count. Yet as this issue arose in the Christ-mysticism of the High Middle Ages, so in the same era there appeared a new subjectivity that reversed the polarity of the whole issue. For Francis of Assisi, who was the apex of the development of Christ-mysticism, was at the same time the fountainhead for a new appreciation of the Historical Jesus of Nazareth as the Divine and Human Model.

I got plenty o' nuthin',
An' nuthin's plenty for me.
—*Ira Gershwin,* Porgy and Bess

11 ✛ The Divine and Human Model

If a pollster were to ask a representative group of informed people, "Which historical figure has most fully embodied the life and teachings of Jesus Christ?" the one mentioned most often would certainly be Francis of Assisi. In him the imitation and obedience of Jesus, in principle binding on every believer, attained a level of fidelity that earned him the designation, confirmed by Pope Pius XI, as "the second Christ."

Little in the early life of Giovanni di Bernardone suggested that he would assume any such place in history. Born to a merchant family in Assisi, he aspired to a chivalric career. Instead, he was converted to be a chevalier of the cross of Christ. His transformation was not one single moment of blinding incandescence but a gradual movement away from his old manner of life to a

new understanding of himself and of his mission. At prayer one day, Francis beheld the crucified Christ, and this vision stayed with him all his life. He understood it to mean that Christ was summoning him personally to "a spirit of poverty, with a deep sense of humility, and an attitude of profound compassion." The summons included the specific instruction to "go and repair my house, which is in total disrepair." At first Francis took this literally, undertaking to repair several nearby church buildings. But it dawned on him that the church to whose rebuilding Christ had called him was nothing less than the very church of Christ on earth. The central content of that mission was disclosed to Francis on 24 February 1209, when he perceived the words of Jesus to have been spoken also to him: "Preach as you go, saying, 'The kingdom of heaven is at hand.' . . . Take no gold, nor silver, nor copper in your belts" (Matt. 10:7, 9). Francis almost immediately began to attract followers, at least three thousand by 1221. The small Church of Santa Maria degli Angeli, popularly called Portiuncula, near Assisi, was one building that Francis restored. It became, in Bonaventure's words, "the place where St. Francis founded the Order of Friars Minor by divine inspiration." (It would also be the place where Francis died on 3 October 1226.)

Francis prepared a monastic rule, which was approved by Pope Innocent III in 1209 or 1210. Neither the pope's approval nor this first *Rule* has survived in written form. It does appear from all accounts that in it Francis avoided lengthy prescriptions of structure or conduct for the order, preferring to "use for the most part the words of the holy Gospel." But that explanation omits the decisive factor: the personality of Francis. Surviving sources compel the conclusion that followers came because of the magnetic pull of Francis and because of the authority of the Gospel of Jesus, and that these two reasons were one in their eyes. For Francis was devoted to what his first biographer, Thomas of Celano, would call "the humility of the incarnation" of Christ.

By far the most dramatic evidence of this identification came near the end of his life, in September 1224. As was his wont, he had gone on retreat to Alvernia, a mountain in Tuscany, where a chapel to Saint Mary of the Angels had been built for the Franciscans. Following the example of Christ in the desert before his temptation (Matt. 4:2), who had in turn followed the example of Moses (Ex. 34:28), Francis spent forty days on the mountain. Then he beheld a seraph with six wings (Isa. 6:1–13), and between its wings he descried the crucified Christ. He was overwhelmed by the vision, and then, in the words of Bonaventure, "as the vision disappeared, it left his heart ablaze with eagerness and impressed upon his body a miraculous likeness. There and then the marks of nails began to appear in his hands and feet, just as he had seen them in the vision of the Man nailed to the Cross. His hands and feet appeared pierced through the center with nails. . . . His right side seemed as if it had been pierced with a lance and was marked with a livid scar which often bled." From the statement of Paul, "I bear on my body the marks [*stigmata*] of Jesus" (Gal. 6:17), these markings were called "stigmata."

Although the cross was one of the most ancient of Christian symbols, often with Christ the King portrayed on it, the depiction of it with the figure of the Crucified did not become the typically Western form until the thirteenth century, the age of Francis of Assisi, and in the opinion of some historians of art and spirituality owes its popularity to Franciscan devotion, as does the crèche. Guido Reni finds a dramatic way of expressing that Franciscan devotion to the crucifix by making the figure of the saint much larger in size but infinitely smaller in importance, as the adoring gaze of Francis takes us to the contemplation of his Divine and Human Model.

In every century, those who have been devoted to Francis of Assisi and those who have painted him have been persuaded that in his life the imitation and obedience of Jesus, in principle binding on every believer, attained a level of fidelity that earned him the designation, confirmed by Pope Pius XI, as "the second Christ."

Francis appears to have been the first person ever to have undergone stigmatization, but there have been other instances of it since. Almost everyone would agree that the stigmatization of Francis was unique, because of the uniqueness of Francis himself as "the second Christ": if it was fitting for anyone ever to bear in his body the stigmata of the sufferings of Christ, Francis was the one to whom it ought to have happened. He himself, it is clear, did not take the stigmata as an occasion for self-esteem; indeed, he even imitated Christ (Matt. 16:20) in keeping his special identity a secret. Nor did he regard them as the primary form of his imitation of Christ. That was a place of honor, or of lack of honor, that belonged to poverty.

Poverty had always been a prominent feature of the kingdom of God as Jesus lived and proclaimed it. "Foxes have holes, and birds of the air have nests," the Gospel of Matthew has Jesus say (Matt. 8:20), "but the Son of man has nowhere to lay his head." The vow of poverty was required by the *Rule* of every monastic order—required of the individual, but not necessarily of the order itself. Throughout the Middle Ages that distinction had been a source of corruption. When monasteries acquired vast holdings that

It had always been a requirement that individual monks embrace poverty, together with chastity and obedience, but the requirement of poverty did not extend to entire monasteries or monastic orders. Francis made a radical break with such ambiguities. He identified poverty as "the queen of the virtues," and he even underwent a "mystic marriage" ceremony, portrayed by Sassetta.

made them rivals of the great noble houses of Europe, satirists and moralists enjoyed contrasting this with the saying of the disciples in the Gospel, "Lo, we have left everything and followed you" (Mark 10:28). Francis made a radical break with these ambiguities. The second written version of his *Rule* described his followers as "strangers and pilgrims in this world," detached from the tyrannical hold of material possessions. With the character in America's best-known folk opera, Francis could have said, "I got plenty o' nuthin',/An' nuthin's plenty for me." Poverty was not merely the absence of property but a positive good, "the queen of the virtues," because of its identification with Christ and with Mary.

It would, however, be a grave error to interpret the Franciscan detachment from material wealth as the expression of a hatred for the material and natural world. Quite the opposite: it was, G. K. Chesterton said, as if Europe had first been obliged to pass through a tunnel of purgation, in which it was cleansed of nature worship, so that then, in Francis, it could come out of the tunnel into the light of God's good sun, cast off the last shreds of the idolatry of nature, and turn to nature. In his familiar *Canticle of Brother Sun*, Francis sang of "Brother Sun": the moon was his sister, the wind his brother; and, in a stanza said to have been added at his last hour, "Sister Death," too, was a gift from God. That regard

A lasting aftereffect of the Franciscan emphasis on the humanity of Jesus was a new appreciation of the nativity; for, in the words of Francis's most important biographer, Thomas of Celano, he "observed the birthday of the Child Jesus with inexpressible eagerness over all other feasts, saying that it was the feast of feasts." In the Lower Church at Assisi (opposite page), Cimabue located the figure of Francis, complete with the stigmata, at the very scene, next to the infant Jesus with his mother and the angels.

As had been the case in a preeminent sense with Christ, so it was also for Francis as "the second Christ" that he shaped subsequent history through his immediate followers. One of these was Bonaventure, the "second founder of the Friars Minor," pictured in the preceding chapter. Another was Anthony of Padua, whom Andrea della Robbia in the Loggia di San Paolo at Florence described in a Franciscan posture with book and flame.

The words of Jesus to Pontius Pilate, "My kingship is not of this world" (John 18:36), served William of Ockham, a Franciscan (subject of this delightful sketch by a student), and Dante Alighieri, who though not a Franciscan was to be buried in a Franciscan habit, as proof that the church of Jesus Christ was most faithful to him when it refused to usurp the political authority of worldly kings and contented itself, as did he, with a spiritual kingship, "not of this world."

for the created world is evident also in the way Francis thought and spoke about the human body. His aspersions on the physical side of human nature were sometimes excessive: he mingled ashes with his food to keep it from being too palatable, and he "would hurl himself into a ditch full of ice" when sexually tempted. Yet the purpose of such self-mortification was to discipline the body for the sake of a higher goal. There are more than superficial similarities between ascetics like Francis and present-day competitive athletes, who grimly strain every muscle, bend every nerve, and punish their bodies—all to win. "They do it to receive a perishable wreath," Francis could say with Paul, "but we an imperishable. . . . I pommel my body and subdue it" (1 Cor. 9:25, 27).

A direct corollary of identifying the sufferings of his body with the sufferings of Christ was a new and deeper awareness of the humanity of Christ, as disclosed in his nativity and sufferings. It was, the followers of Francis believed, as if "the Child Jesus had been forgotten in the hearts of many" but "was brought to life again through his servant St. Francis." The celebration of Christmas had come rather late in the development of the Christian calendar. But Francis, according to Thomas of Celano, "observed the birthday of the Child Jesus with inexpressible eagerness over all other feasts, saying that it was the feast of feasts." As a contribution to the observance of this festival—and, by serendipity, to the history of art—Francis in 1223 set up a *presepio,* or crèche, at the Umbrian village of Greccio. But his most lasting impression in the histories of art and of devotion came

through his concentration on the Jesus of the cross. He made his own the determination "to know nothing except Jesus Christ and him crucified" (1 Cor. 2:2), and strove to imitate Christ perfectly in life and in death. The experience of Francis as the second Christ, and specifically of his conformity to the Christ of the cross, endowed painting and poetry with a new realism, as artists and writers struggled to give form to the fundamental conviction that in the suffering and death of Jesus on the cross the mystery both of divine life and of human life became manifest.

Yet it was not conformity to Christ in his crucifixion but conformity to Christ in his poverty, that became the most controversial item on the Franciscan agenda. After Francis's death, some of the Franciscan "Spirituals," combining his insistence on a strict construction of poverty with a denunciation of the church for its compromises, saw themselves as the forerunners of a new "spiritual church," in which the purity of the Gospel, as announced by Francis the "angel with an eternal Gospel" (Rev. 14:6), would be restored and absolute poverty would prevail. The more moderate "Conventuals" refrained from posing such a radical antithesis between the institutional church and the "spiritual church." They found their most balanced interpreter in Bonaventure, whose normative reinterpretation of the *Rule* and authorized *Life* of Francis made Franciscanism acceptable to the church and made Bonaventure, as he is often called, the "second founder of the Friars Minor."

"Let our sovereign study be—in the life of Jesu Christ." This opening theme of Thomas à Kempis, The Imitation of Christ, *shown here in a German translation published in 1539, plays itself out in infinite variations throughout the work. Each stage in "the life of Jesu Christ" corresponded to a stage in the life of his follower, from birth to death to resurrection, from humility to glory.*

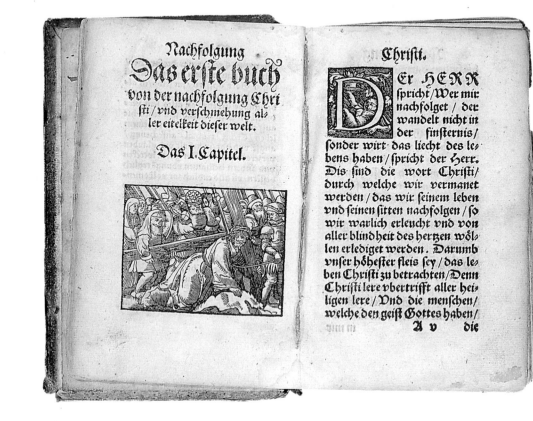

This controversy over poverty had some unlooked-for political consequences. Nothing would seem to be more otherworldly and apolitical—indeed, downright idealistic—than the doctrine that because Christ, Mary, and the apostles had practiced total poverty, it was incumbent on the church to obey their example and to abstain from owning anything. Ironically, this otherworldly position became allied with the assertion of the authority of the state against the church. The Franciscan William of Ockham attacked Pope John XXII for modifying the requirements of the *Rule* and *Testament* of Francis on poverty. During the ensuing conflict, Ockham found political asylum in 1328 at the court of the Holy Roman Emperor, Louis IV "the Bavarian," who was engaged in a struggle with the papacy over the relative prerogatives of church and state. Adapting some of Ockham's arguments in a manner that Ockham had not intended, the emperor and his supporters cast themselves as liberators of the true church from the burdens of property and power. In the process, then, this image of Jesus contributed to the formulation of the founding principles and "secular values" of modern political philosophy. This was a long distance indeed from the Francis of the stigmata and his quest for the simplicity of the life set forth in the Gospels.

Even amid the political turbulence of the later Middle Ages, that quest for the authenticity of the Gospels continued to exercise its hold upon human hearts and lives. Early in the fifteenth century there appeared an anonymous book, *The Imitation of Christ,* which is often said to have achieved a greater circulation than any book in history save the Bible. It is generally attributed to the Rhenish mystic Thomas à Kempis. "Ever put before thee," it admonished (in a sixteenth-century English translation), "the image of the crucifix"; and it exclaimed, quite in the spirit of Francis: "Would God we had naught else to do, but only to praise our Lord Jesus Christ with all our heart." In its first chapter it announced: "Let our sovereign study be—in the life of Jesu Christ." That study was the foundation both of an accurate self-knowledge and of a true recognition of the reality of God. Nor was it enough to know the church's doctrines or the sayings of the Bible, "for whoever will understand the words of Christ plainly and in their full savour must study to conform all his life to his life." Once again, the Franciscan glorification of Jesus as the Divine and Human Model was asserting itself as an alternative to the smugness of conventional religion.

And it goes on doing so. During the year 1926, the seven-hundredth anniversary of the death of Francis, two million pilgrims came to Assisi. Most were devout members of the church, who believed, as had Bonaventure and Francis, that loyalty to the institutional church and the imitation of Christ were not incompatible but mutually supportive and ultimately identical. And yet Francis has also become the patron saint of the growing number who have become more devoted to Jesus as they have become more alienated from the church. The interpreter of Francis who has had the widest influence among secular moderns has not been Bonaventure but Paul Sabatier, a French Protestant theologian who believed that the original message of Francis had been expurgated by later disciples to make him acceptable to church authorities.

That ambiguity runs through the entire history of Francis and of the Franciscan spirit. It is the theme of one of the oldest of the innumerable legends about Saint Francis. When Francis came to Rome to obtain the pope's sanction for a new religious order, Pope Innocent III was deeply touched by the sanctity of Francis and by the power of his evangelical commitment, but he withheld any response until he could consult the cardinals. Some of them expressed misgivings about Francis, particularly about the parallels between the preachments of various heretical movements abroad in the land and his message of radical poverty in obedience to Christ the Divine and Human Model. Others were

Spiritual movements, including the one that bears the name of Christ, have often become the victims of their own success. Already during his lifetime, Francis achieved a notoriety that threatened to engulf him and his ideal of poverty in a sea of popularity. To his millions of followers, the fortresslike Basilica of Saint Francis at Assisi incarnates the paradox in wood and stone; and yet somehow those followers have been able to learn, and even to follow, the ideals and the simplicity of Francis even when they came as pilgrims to Assisi.

more positive in their reactions. Ultimately, of course, the decision was up to the pope. The following night Pope Innocent III had a dream of a young man attired in coarse cloth, but with his right hand holding up the Basilica of Saint John Lateran, which was in danger of falling over until this young man came to its rescue. On the basis of the vision in the dream, the pope granted the request and confirmed the first *Rule.*

The contrast could not have been more striking. Here was the most powerful man to occupy the Throne of Saint Peter, before or since. A man of blameless character and great eloquence, Innocent III believed that the pope was "less than God but more than man," mediating between them. At the greatest church council of the Middle Ages, held in 1215 at the Lateran, he was hailed as "lord of the world." The continuity of the church, without which, historically speaking, there would be no Gospel—and no Francis of Assisi—and the presence and power of Christ became visible, almost tangible, in the pontificate of Pope Innocent III. And there was the simple figure of the young man from Assisi, who has taken on one shoulder the entire weight of the Lateran—and of the world.

And the question we must ask, though we may not be able to answer it, is: Now which of the two was truly the "Vicar of Christ"?

The Vision of Innocent III graphically embodies the alternate interpretations, prevalent since the early church, of the words of the Gospel (Matt. 16:18), in which, speaking to Peter ("the man of the rock"), Christ promised to build his church "on this rock." Did "rock" here refer to Peter and his successors (therefore to Innocent III as pope) or to the faith that Peter had just confessed in Christ as "the Son of the living God" (therefore to Francis as "the second Christ")?

Know then thyself, presume not God to scan,
The proper study of mankind is man.
—*Alexander Pope,* An Essay on Man

12 ✥ The Universal Man

"The Discovery of the World and of Man" and "The Development of the Individual" were, according to the founder of modern Renaissance studies, Jacob Burckhardt, two major themes of the Renaissance. But the very concept and name *Renaissance,* whatever the ultimate origins of the idea may have been, had come into the vocabulary of European civilization principally through the teachings of Jesus. "Unless one is born anew [*renatus*]," Jesus declared, "he cannot see the kingdom of God" (John 3:3). And in the Book of Revelation (21:5) he said, "Behold, I make all things new." Although they contrasted the "new birth" of the Renaissance with the "Gothic" decadence of the Middle Ages, Renaissance humanists yielded to no medieval theologian in their admiration for Jesus and their devotion to him. "What else is the philosophy of Christ," Eras-

mus asked in the preface to his Greek New Testament in 1516, "which He Himself calls a 'rebirth [*renascentia*],' than the restoration of [human] nature to the original goodness of its creation?" Therefore, the Renaissance was a rebirth not only of art and literature but of religious faith. The Renaissance title "Universal Man," which has come to be known as the slogan of the Renaissance and which the humanists not only employed but strove to embody, may well serve as a summary of the place that Renaissance thought and art accorded to Jesus, as the only one who could be, and had always been, called that in the strict and total sense.

The nineteenth-century effort to see the Renaissance as a naturalistic revolt against traditional ideas of Christ seems to have stemmed from Goethe, who characterized Leonardo's portrayal of Jesus as "the boldest attempt to adhere to nature, while, at the same time, the object is supernatural," with the result that "the majesty, the uncontrolled will, the power and might of the Deity" were not expressed. Walter Pater similarly set forth the conclusion that "though [Leonardo] handles sacred subjects continually, he is the most profane of painters," so that in *The Last Supper* an aestheticist naturalism strove "to see the Eucharist, not as the pale Host of the altar, but as one taking leave of his friends."

More recently, however, historians of Renaissance thought such as Charles Trinkaus and historians of Renaissance art such as Leo Steinberg have come to interpret this supposed naturalism more subtly and profoundly. Steinberg has related the sexuality of Jesus in Renaissance art to the doctrine of the incarnation as "the centrum of Christian orthodoxy." Unlike many of its predecessors in Christian history, "Renaissance culture not only advanced an incarnational theology (as the Greek Church had also done), but evolved representational modes adequate to its expression." Therefore, Steinberg concludes, "we may take Renaissance art to be the first and last phase of Christian art that can claim full Christian orthodoxy."

A representative spokesman for this Renaissance view of the Universal Man was the humanist and statesman Donato Acciaiuoli, who set his exposition of the Eucharist apart from the "many subtle investigations which the [scholastic] doctors have made concerning its matter, its form, its efficient cause and its final cause, and how the substance of the bread and the wine is transformed into the most true body of Christ." But it would be a serious anachronism to read such a polemic as a rejection of orthodox doctrine, which Acciaiuoli reaffirmed even as he broke with the scholastic version of it. The Eucharist was

Although a secularizing interpretation of Renaissance painters professed to find in their pictorial reenactments of the Last Supper a break with traditional views of Christ and an effort "to see the Eucharist, not as the pale Host of the altar, but as one taking leave of his friends," closer examination documents their continuing reverence for Jesus Christ, as in the painting by Ghirlandaio (opposite page). Leonardo's treatment (above) catches the response of the disciples to the sublime person of their Lord when, "as they were eating, he said, 'Truly, I say to you, one of you will betray me'" (Matt. 26:21).

for Donato, as Trinkaus has put it, "the most important mode by which Christ reinforces faith in his doctrine, as it is a commemoration of the divine Incarnation by which and through which Christ became the great teacher of mankind." Jesus was "the teacher and exemplar," an image of him in which Donato Acciaiuoli joined himself to the Franciscan revival of the Gospel portrait and to the Jesus who had been celebrated earlier in the same century by the *Imitation of Christ* of Thomas à Kempis. It is, then, "difficult and essentially arbitrary either to separate the humanists' views of human nature from their peculiar approaches to religion [above all, their picture of Jesus], or on the other hand to do the reverse." With their latter-day Catholic disciple Alexander Pope, the humanists believed that "the proper study of mankind is man," but they found that study of mankind fulfilled in the Universal Man.

Dante Alighieri occupies an important place in the history of the Renaissance image of Jesus, as he does in every other aspect of the Renaissance, for which, in Burckhardt's words, "in all essential points. . . the first witness to be called is Dante," perhaps most eloquently in Burckhardt's exposition of the very ideal of *l'uomo universale,* the Universal Man. Yet to a degree that Burckhardt did not adequately appreciate, Dante's inspiration for both poetry and politics was inseparable from the person of Jesus, as in the very title of Dante's first book, the *Vita Nuova.* In this book Dante is told that Giovanna, the sweetheart of his "first friend," Guido Cavalcanti, has the nickname Primavera (Spring) because, as the forerunner of Beatrice, "prima verrà [she will come first]," and she is called Giovanna in honor of John the Baptist, who likewise came first as the one sent to announce the coming of Christ. Beatrice herself, therefore, as the very incarnation of love, is, in the phrase of Charles Singleton, a translator of the *Divine Comedy* into English, "an analogy and a metaphor of Christ."

If that is what Beatrice is "already in the *Vita Nuova,*" then she becomes, as Thomas Bergin puts it, "in the *Commedia,* a symbol of theology, learning illuminated by grace, even the Christian faith." Near the end of the *Purgatorio* she promises Dante that he will be "with me forever a citizen of that Rome where Christ is a 'Roman,' " that is, of Paradise. As the poet's "sweet and dear guide," Beatrice has the function of leading him—and the reader—to Christ and to the Mother of Christ, who are always inseparable and sometimes (but by no means always) well-nigh indistinguishable. In the words of Beatrice to Dante that follow, Mary is "the rose in which the divine Word was made flesh," but like all the other flowers in the divine "garden," she, too, "blossoms under the rays of Christ," not finally of her own powers. For even while he is transported by the rhapsody to Mary, he describes her countenance as "the face that most resembles Christ." It is amid the strains of a hymn to the Queen of Heaven, the *Regina coeli,* that Peter and the church triumphant receive their "treasure" of "victory, under the exalted Son of God and of Mary." With her eyes she directs the poet's attention to "the eternal Light," by which she, too, is illumined,

and to eternal Love, by which she too is saved and sustained, the Light and the Love that have come solely through Jesus, the Universal Man, Son of God and Son of Mary.

Dante also drew on the figure of Jesus for his political theory. He was, as a Ghibelline, a supporter of the rights of the empire against the temporal claims of the papacy. The theological justification for the temporal claims of the papacy was the giving of the keys of the kingdom of heaven by Christ to Peter, so that "whatever [*quodcunque*]" he would bind and loose here on earth, be it in church or state, would also be bound and loosed in

The parallel and the contrast between "sacred" and "secular" painting in the Renaissance achieves dramatic, even shocking, expression in two works of Sandro Botticelli, The Mystic Nativity *and* The Birth of Venus. *The first is so devout and inward-looking that interpreters of Botticelli still puzzle over what he was trying to say about his own "mystical" life in describing the birth of Christ. The birth of Venus, by contrast, is "the first monumental image since Roman times of the nude goddess in a pose derived from the classical statues of Venus." Each is true to its subject, but each is apparently true to Botticelli's complicated artistic spirit as well.*

heaven (Matt. 16:18–19). But Dante insisted that Christ had not intended this "whatever" to be taken "absolutely" but had meant that it "must be related to a particular class of things"—namely, the authority to grant absolution and forgiveness. Although the biblical doctrine of the creation of a single humanity in the image of God implied that a single world government would be best, this did not mean that the papacy should have both spiritual and temporal authority or that it should function as such a world government. Man was created for a twofold goal, "the bliss of this life . . . and the bliss of eternal life." The bliss of eternal life was the gift and achievement of Christ and of his suffering, but in the very midst of the suffering the same Christ had declared to Pontius Pilate: "My kingship is not of this world" (John 18:36).

According to Dante, this was not to be taken, as a later secularism would contend, "as if Christ, who is God, were not lord of this world"; rather, it meant that "as an example for

Both the myth of the origin of the Milky Way from the milk of Juno's breast and the Gospel narrative of the entombment of Christ after the crucifixion engaged Tintoretto's attention in late life. The similarities in the treatment of the two themes—naked limbs pointed diagonally across the center of the painting, with the clothing draped to set them off—nevertheless do not obscure the differences in both purpose and mood: the bearded figure of Joseph of Arimathea in the Entombment *is a self-portrait of the artist, who does not depict himself in the mythological painting.*

the Church," he would not exercise dominion over the kingdoms of this world. It would, then, be fair to Dante's position in the *De Monarchia* to say that what was at issue for him was the relation between two authoritative sets of sayings of Jesus, and the familiar hermeneutical problem of deciding which sayings were to be interpreted in the light of which. It was, he was arguing, most faithful to the will of God as articulated in the life and teachings of Jesus to let the church be the church and to let the empire be the empire, and not to subordinate the essential character of either to the other. Moreover, as Ernst Kantorowicz has carefully observed, "A duality of goals does not necessarily imply a conflict of loyalties or even an antithesis. There is no antithesis of 'human' versus 'Christian' in the work of Dante, who wrote as a Christian and addressed himself to a Christian society, and who, in the last passage of the *Monarchy,* said clearly that 'after a certain fashion [*quodammodo*] this mortal blessedness is ordained toward an immortal blessedness.' " For that teaching, too, his highest authority was the revelation in Jesus Christ.

Nevertheless, most Renaissance scholars would probably concur in the judgment of Paul Oskar Kristeller that "if we try to assess the positive contributions of humanist

scholarship to Renaissance theology, we must emphasize above all their achievements in what might be called sacred philology." "Sacred philology" in this sense participated in the more general "revival of antiquity," as Burckhardt calls it, in which the humanists of the Renaissance were caught up. "Had it not been for the enthusiasm of a few collectors of that age," Burckhardt suggests, "who shrank from no effort or privation in their researches, we should certainly possess only a small part of the literature, especially of the Greeks, which is now in our hands." The zeal for the literature of classical antiquity was more than nostalgia or acquisitiveness, though both of these were undoubtedly present. It was grounded in the conviction that a major source for the superficiality and the superstition of the present was an ignorance of the classical past and that therefore a recovery of that past would serve as an antidote. "Ad fontes!" was the watchword: "Back to the sources!" Although these classical "sources" were in both Latin and Greek, with Cicero being perhaps the most important single author, the great innovation introduced by Renaissance humanism was an interest in the study of Greek.

The scholarly methods of sacred philology were applied not only to classical philosophers, poets, and dramatists, but to the church fathers and above all to the one ancient text that everyone was eager to learn to read, the Greek New Testament. The reappropriation of the Greek New Testament by Western scholars in the Renaissance of the fifteenth and sixteenth centuries brought on a systematic philological review. Pioneering this campaign was the Italian scholar Lorenzo Valla, whose *Annotations on the New Testament* consisted of grammatical and philological notes on various texts. Thus he concluded that the summons with which the preaching of Jesus began did not say, as medieval misreading had supposed, "Do penance [*Poenitentiam agite*]," but "Repent," that is, "Turn your mind around" (Matt. 3:2); and the salutation of the angel to the Virgin Mary, *kecharitōmenē* in Greek, did not mean "full of grace [*gratia plena*]," as the Ave Maria in the Vulgate had it, but "highly favored" (Luke 1:28).

Erasmus of Rotterdam elevated the recovery of the original message of Jesus, on the basis of the Greek sources, into a comprehensive program of church reform and theological renaissance. He did so in 1505, when he published Valla's *Annotations on the New Testament* with a preface of his own that has been called "Erasmus' Inaugural Lecture as Professor-at-large to Christendom." Theology, he insisted, had to be founded on grammar. The original Greek New Testament had to be freed of the mistranslations in the Vulgate, the misinterpretations imposed upon it by later theologians, and the corruptions of the text introduced by copyists. To that end Erasmus in 1516 edited the first printed edition of the Greek New Testament to be published, revolutionizing forever the image of Jesus in Western culture. Erasmus used sacred philology to discover and recover *philosophia Christi*, "the philosophy of Christ," which he expounded most eloquently in his *Enchiridion* of 1503. Its central theme was: "Make Christ the only goal of your life. Dedicate to Him

Drawn by leading artists, including Hans Holbein the Younger (ca. 1523), and rightly acclaimed by his contemporaries as the greatest scholar of his age for producing first editions of the ancient classics as well as of the fathers of the early church, Erasmus of Rotterdam was also the author of several best-sellers, such as his Enchiridion of the Christian Soldier of 1503, which urged: "Make Christ the only goal of your life." And as he lay dying in 1536, he prayed, "O Jesu misericordia, O Jesus, have mercy."

The most influential book to be produced in the Renaissance was not, as some might suppose, Machiavelli's Prince *but the first published edition of the Greek New Testament, the* Novum Instrumentum, *produced by Erasmus in 1516, which made the original text accessible to many for the first time. This edition and its successors became the basis for literally thousands of new translations of the Gospels into most of the languages of the earth, and, contrary to Erasmus's intentions, it also helped set off the Reformation.*

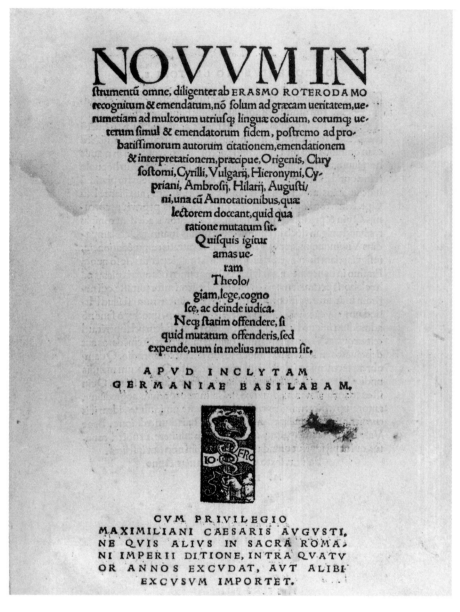

all your enthusiasm, all your effort, your leisure as well as your business. And don't look upon Christ as a mere word, as an empty expression, but rather as charity, simplicity, patience and purity—in short, in terms of everything he has taught us." For Jesus was "the sole archetype of godliness."

The authentic Jesus, then, was the Jesus of the Gospels, whose life and teachings were to be studied on the basis of the original sources in the Greek New Testament. In the conclusion of the *Enchiridion,* Erasmus defended the combination of *philosophia Christi* and Christian humanism against "certain detractors who think that true religion has nothing to do with the humanities [*bonae literae*]" or with "a knowledge of Greek and Latin." To the contrary, it was precisely through the humanistic study of the Gospels, using the same literary methods and philological scholarship that Erasmus's fellow humanists were applying to other texts of classical antiquity, that the reader could discover the meaning of the Gospels and thus learn the "words of life" spoken by Jesus, which "flowed from a soul that was never for a moment separated from the divinity and that alone restores us to everlasting life."

In his effort to disentangle the person and message of Jesus from the complications imposed by the scholastic theologians, Erasmus harked back to what Etienne Gilson has called the "Christian Socratism" of various early Christian writers. For as "the author of wisdom and Himself Wisdom in person, the true Light, who alone shatters the night of earthly folly," Jesus Christ had taught that "the crown of wisdom is that you know yourself," as Socrates (and, centuries later, Alexander Pope) taught. His message, therefore, was a revelation from God himself. And yet Erasmus could also make the appeal: "The way of Christ is the most sensible and logical one to follow. . . . When you abandon the world for Christ, you do not give up anything. Rather, you exchange it for something far better. You change silver into gold, and rocks into precious gems." In keeping with this Christian Socratism, he could "recommend the Platonists most highly" among all the classics, because "not only their ideas but their very mode of expression approaches that of the Gospels."

This apparent equation of the *philosophia Christi* with pagan philosophy persuaded Martin Luther that Erasmus was not serious in his espousal of the biblical message, but was essentially an "Epicurus." Historians who have followed Luther in this judgment have not only misread Erasmus but have borne false witness against him: "the fool's part, mistaken for pagan frivolity in serious times, has betrayed Erasmus." For when he died on 12 July 1536, Erasmus, faithful to the *philosophia Christi* and to the church founded by Jesus the Universal Man—not as the church was, but as Jesus had intended it to be—received the sacraments of that church, the chrism of anointing and the food for his final journey in the *viaticum,* and died with a prayer to Jesus on his lips, which he repeated over and over again: *O Jesu misericordia; Domine libera me,* "O Jesus, have mercy; Lord deliver me."

Did we in our own strength confide, Our striving would be losing;

Were not the right Man on our side, the Man of God's own choosing.

Dost ask who that may be? Christ Jesus, it is he;

Lord Sabaoth his Name, From age to age the same,

And he must win the battle.

—Martin Luther, A Mighty Fortress Is Our God

  (tr. Frederick H. Hedge)

13 ✣ The Mirror of the Eternal

The Reformation began with an appeal from the authority of the institutional church to that of the Historical Jesus. On 31 October 1517 Martin Luther posted his ninety-five theses, the first of which read: "In the Name of Our Lord Jesus Christ. Amen. When our Lord and Master Jesus Christ said, 'Repent [*Poenitentiam agite*]' (Matt. 4:17), he willed the entire life of believers to be one of repentance." This was a direct application of the sacred philology of Christian humanism to the sacramental life of the church. Luther became the Reformer, he tells us, when he was pondering the meaning of Paul's words (Rom. 1:17), "In [the gospel] the righteousness of God is revealed through faith for faith; as it is written, 'He who through faith is righteous shall live.'" How could it be the content of the gospel of Christ, as "good news," that God was a righteous judge,

rewarding the good and punishing the evil? Then he suddenly broke through to the insight that the "righteousness of God" here was not the righteousness by which God *was* righteous in himself (passive righteousness) but instead the righteousness by which, for Christ's sake, God *made* sinners righteous (active righteousness) through justification. When he made that discovery, Luther said, it was as though the gates of Paradise had opened.

What Luther and the other Reformers learned from Paul was above all "to know nothing . . . except Jesus Christ and him crucified" (1 Cor. 2:2). Jesus was the "Mirror of the fatherly heart [of God], apart from whom we see nothing but a wrathful and terrible judge." For John Calvin likewise, "Christ is the Mirror wherein we must, and without self-deception may, contemplate our own election." "Let Christ," said an official Reformed confession, "be the Mirror in which we contemplate our predestination." "Mirror" was, then, a key metaphor in Reformation thought, central both to the religious achievements of the Reformation and to its cultural contributions. The Reformers would all have agreed in principle with the universal consensus that Jesus, as the Mirror of the Eternal, was the revelation of the True, the Beautiful, and the Good (though they might not all have liked such terminology). Yet it was only on his significance as Mirror of the True that the "magisterial Reformers" would have found anything approaching substantial agreement: in the words of Luther's best-known hymn, Christ, "the Man of God's own choosing," was at the same time "the Lord Sabaoth," the true revelation of "the hidden God," and the source of divine Truth as this had been set down in the Scriptures. Quoting the words of the New Testament, "the light of the knowledge of the glory of God in the face of Jesus Christ" (2 Cor. 4:6), Calvin explained that "when [God] appeared in this, his image, he, as it were, made himself visible; whereas his appearance had before been indistinct and shadowed."

As Karl Holl has said, however, "the Reformation, in fact, enriched all areas of culture." Principal among these were, on one hand, literature, art, and music, inspired by Jesus as Mirror of the Beautiful, and, on the other, the social and political order, illumined by Jesus as Mirror of the Good. But Calvin and his followers were suspicious of the idolatrous possibilities in the former, while Luther and his followers were extremely hesitant about the political implications of the latter. The cultural and social relevance of these differences over the precise meaning of Jesus as Mirror, which are certainly related to theological differences, has had an even more far-reaching effect on the history of the past four centuries.

Luther's most important literary achievement was his translation of the New Testament into German, published in September 1522. It was to go through about one hundred separate editions in his own lifetime, and has undergone innumerable ones since. Heinrich Bornkamm, who has given special study to Luther as translator, speaks of "the difference between the eaglelike flight of Luther's language and the diction of his medieval pre-

decessors," adding that "a wonderful providence had placed Luther, the greatest sculptor of the German language," into just the right time and place to make his historic contribution to the creation of modern German. The various Reformation translations of the Bible into the vernacular became turning points for their languages, a process that has continued, with additional languages, ever since.

Luther applied himself to reconstructing the history of the Jesus of the Gospels and making him live for his hearers. The comment of the German poet Heinrich Heine that Luther, "who could scold like a fishwife, could also be as gentle as a sensitive maiden," is nowhere more apt than in Luther's translation and paraphrases of the Gospels. Far from transposing the language of the Gospels into the key of the Pauline epistles, as some scholars claim, he endeavored to allow each evangelist, or rather Jesus according to each evangelist, to speak in a distinctive accent. The outcome was a freshness of language that made Jesus a sixteenth-century contemporary. To hearers who clucked sentimentally over the poverty of the Infant Jesus, "If only I had been there! How quick I would have been to help the Baby!" Luther retorted: "Why don't you do it now? You have Christ in your neighbor." The admonition to consider the lilies of the field and the birds of the air (Matt.

As he desperately sought, in an intense personal crisis, for the authentic meaning and message of Jesus Christ, the thought and experience of Martin Luther (whose portrait Lucas Cranach the Elder painted in 1526) converged with the deepest needs and longings of an era. The explosive result of that convergence was the Protestant Reformation, with its passionate insistence on Christ as the Mirror of the Eternal, to whom tradition, church, and even Scripture were to be subordinated.

6:26–28) became at Luther's hands a discourse about how Jesus "is making the birds our schoolmasters and teachers. It is a great and abiding disgrace to us that in the Gospel a helpless sparrow should become a theologian and a preacher to the wisest of men." In Calvin's exegesis, too, the scenes of the Gospel story acquired directness and challenging force, as in his vivid exposition of the encounter between Jesus and the woman at the well recounted in the fourth chapter of the Gospel of John.

Luther strove to infuse into the religious art of the later Middle Ages his understanding of what the authentic message of the Gospels was: it was specifically the humanity of Jesus that was the Mirror of the Eternal. Albrecht Dürer shared these ideas and reflected them in his art; his biographer speaks of "a conversion—both in subject matter and in style" brought about in Dürer's faith and life through his acceptance of Luther's teachings, as a consequence of which, the art historian Erwin Panofsky says, "the man who had

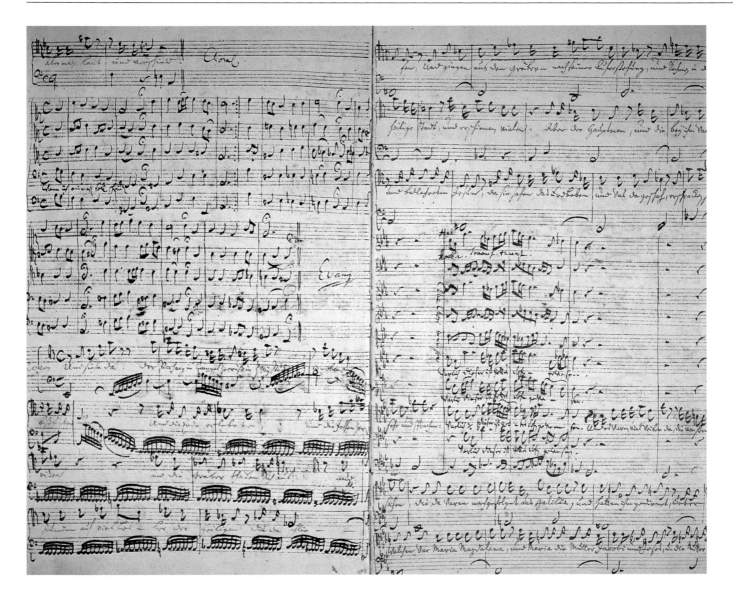

done more than any other to familiarize the Northern world with the true spirit of pagan Antiquity now practically abandoned secular subject matter except for scientific illustrations, traveler's records and portraiture."

As the philosopher of culture Wilhelm Dilthey has observed, the true significance of Luther and the Reformation "cannot be fully appreciated merely on the basis of works of dogmatics. Its documents are the writings of Luther, the church chorale, the sacred music of Bach and Handel, and the structure of community life in the church." Some Reformation groups objected to the creation of vernacular hymns, preferring to rely on paraphrases of "God's hymnbook," the Psalter, and producing such masterworks as the *Geneva Psalter* and the *Bay Psalm Book.* But Luther was "not of the opinion that the gospel should destroy and blight all the arts, as some of the pseudo-religious claim." He would, he added, "like to see all the arts, especially music, used in the service of Him who

The Christ-centered spirituality of the Reformation expressed itself in many forms, but nowhere more profoundly than in the Saint Matthew Passion *of Johann Sebastian Bach. The objectivity of the death of Christ as (in the opening children's chorus) "the Lamb of God" who bore the sins of the entire human race (John 1:29) comes together with the delicate subjectivity of the individual soul as it prays to Christ (in these words of the original score), "Be near me when I am dying!"*

During the sixteenth century the renewed sense of Jesus as the Mirror of the Eternal was not confined to Protestantism but was equally central to the Catholic Reformation. Writing a masterpiece of spirituality entitled The Names of Christ, *the Spanish Catholic Reformer Luis de León exalted "Jesus' spirit" as one that "penetrates and changes" all those it touches. For "in Jesus Christ, as in a deep well, as in a vast ocean, we find a treasure of Being."*

gave and made them." Taking up and developing the style of hymns and chorales that had arisen during the later Middle Ages, Luther gave them new life, and the chorale, as it reached its pinnacle in the work of such poets and composers as Paul Gerhardt, became one of the principal cultural monuments of the Reformation. It was Bach's genius to bring together, in the cantatas and then on a larger scale in the *Passions,* these two Reformation elements: the text of the Gospel in Luther's unmatched translation and the chorale. Now hearers could experience the meaning of the life and death of Jesus as Mirror of the Eternal with unmatched freshness and power. In the words of Archbishop Nathan Söderblom of Sweden, "The Passion music . . . constitutes in its way the most important addition that has ever been made to the sources of revelation in the Old and New Testament. If you ask about a fifth Gospel, I do not hesitate to name the interpretation of salvation history as it reached its acme in Johann Sebastian Bach."

The contemporaneity of Christ was likewise the central theme of one of the masterpieces of the Catholic Reformation in Spain, *The Names of Christ* by Luis de León. "The names which Scriptures give to Christ," he says, "are numerous, like his virtues and attributes." "Jesus' spirit," he writes, "penetrates and changes" the human soul and the human personality; for "in Jesus Christ, as in a deep well, as in a vast ocean, we find a treasure of Being." That treasure had brought "beauty" and "virtue" through "the new laws given to us by Jesus." It was the purpose and the fulfillment of human life to find the treasure and to live in obedience to the "new laws."

Such Christ-mysticism achieved even greater heights of both spirituality and literary

EL MFR. LUIS DE LEON

LEX

GRATIA

MYSTERIUM IVSTIFICATIONIS

PECCATVM

AGNVS DEI

HOMO

MORS

VICTORIA NOSTRA

MISIT DEVS HOMO
QVIS ME ERIPIET EX
HOC CORPORE MORTI
OB NOXIO RO 7

ESAYAS PROPHETA
ECCE VIRGO CONCIPIET ET PARIET FILIVM . ISA . 7

IOANNES BAPTISTA
ECCE AGNVS ILLE DEI QVI TOLLIT PECCATV MVDI . IOA

The theme of Hans Holbein's Allegory of the Old and New Testaments *is the contrast expressed by the Gospel of John (1:17), "The law was given through Moses; grace and truth came through Jesus Christ"—the first of these depicted at the far upper left, the second at the far lower right. Not incidentally, because Luther criticized Roman Catholicism for confusing the gospel with the law, this* Allegory *was likewise intended as a vindication of the Reformation doctrine.*

power in the sixteenth-century poems of the Spanish mystic Saint John of the Cross. He was both a poet and a philosopher, schooled in the thought of Thomas Aquinas, striving to resolve the tensions between intellect and will, between the knowledge of God and the love of God. The resolution came in Jesus as Mirror of the Eternal. In his *Songs of the Soul,* he explored "the path of spiritual negation," which had been charted by the Christian Neoplatonists. But knowledge of Christ, even this knowledge through negation, was not in itself sufficient: love of Christ had to follow. In the madrigal "Of Christ and the Soul," he described the predicament of a young lover, "with love in his heart like a ruinous wound," as a metaphor for the mystical love between the soul and Christ. The two themes of knowledge and love converged in his ballad "On the Incarnation," a conversation be-tween Jesus and his heavenly Father about the mystical earthly bride whom the Father had found for him. "Perfect love" would be fulfilled in the union between this bride and Jesus, the Mirror of the Eternal.

By contrast, when it came to defining Jesus as the Mirror of the Good for the political order, Luther drew the line against seeking to make the person and message of Jesus con-

"Of Christ and the Soul"
was the title of a madrigal in which
Saint John of the Cross poured out
the mystical love between the soul
and Christ. And in "The Dark
Night of the Soul" he reinterpreted
the traditional steps of the mystic
ascent of the soul to Christ.
Salvador Dali boldly imitated the
mystical poet in his painting
The Christ of Saint John
of the Cross.

In 1555, nine years after Luther's
death, an altarpiece by Lucas
Cranach the Younger (opposite
page) was dedicated in Weimar, for
which, like countless medieval
artists before him, Cranach had
painted the Crucifixion of Christ.
But suddenly, a second look at the
painting discovers that the most
prominent of the figures gathered at
the foot of the cross is, unmistak-
ably, Martin Luther—not Christ's
contemporary but Holbein's, but
made contemporary to Christ by
the word and the sacraments.

temporary or relevant in any direct way. In expounding the entire Sermon on the Mount in his sermons of 1530–32, Luther attacked those "who have failed to distinguish properly between the secular and the spiritual, between the kingdom of Christ and the kingdom of the world." Jesus here "is not tampering with the responsibility and authority of the government, but teaching his individual Christians how to live personally, apart from their official position and authority." For "there is no getting around it, a Christian has to be a secular person of some sort." As such, the Christian was not to attempt to use the teachings of Jesus or the laws of the Bible to govern the state. That was best done on the basis not of revelation but of reason, by the legislation of "the mirror of the Saxons [*Sachsenspiegel*]," not by the decrees of Jesus, the Mirror of the Eternal. Jesus forbade taking oaths, the government required it; and both were right, each in the proper sphere. The Gospels did not, as such, provide any special insight into the specifics of what it meant to rule justly. Therefore, politically involved though he and his Reformation undoubtedly were,

John Calvin belonged to the second generation of Protestant Reformers, whose historic task it was to systematize and consolidate the achievements of the first generation. This he did above all in the Swiss city and canton of Geneva, where he was the dominant presence from 1541 to 1564. In recognition of this and in observance of his quadricentennial, Geneva in 1909–17 raised statues to the Reformers—Calvin, Guillaume Farel, Théodore de Bèze, and John Knox—but Calvin does manage to stand out from the rest.

Luther did not evolve a "Christian politics," for that was not why Jesus Christ had come to earth.

For the articulation of a Christian politics in the age of the Reformation, and one that would fundamentally redefine the nature of government especially in the English-speaking world, we must look not to Luther's Wittenberg but to Calvin's Geneva. Calvin acknowledged "that Christ's spiritual Kingdom and the civil jurisdiction are things completely distinct." But he went on to assert: "Civil government has as its appointed end, so long as we live among men, to cherish and protect the outward worship of God, to defend sound doctrine of piety and the position of the church, to adjust our life to the society of men, to form our social behavior to civil righteousness, to reconcile us with one another, and to promote general peace and tranquillity." Magistrates, therefore, were to "submit to Christ the power with which they have been invested, that He [Jesus Christ] alone may tower over all."

But if the government was to achieve faithfulness to Christ as the Mirror of the Good, it was essential that the word of God be preached and taught in all its truth and purity and be applied concretely to the total life of the individual and of society. In principle, to be sure, the Reformation idea of the universal priesthood of all believers meant that not only the clergy but also the laity had the capacity to read, understand, and apply the

teachings of the Bible. Yet sacred philology often contradicted the universal priesthood: the Bible had to be understood on the basis of the authentic original text, in Hebrew and Greek, which, most of the time, only clergy and theologians could comprehend properly. Thus the scholarly authority of the Reformation clergy replaced the priestly authority of the medieval clergy. Functionally, therefore, the quest for a form of government that would embody the will that God had revealed for society in Jesus Christ the Mirror led to a system that has often been called by the ambiguous term *theocracy*.

When Calvin's followers finally established a society in which it was possible to carry out the duty to shape society on the basis of the law of Christ, the underlying assumption of that society was that the law of Christ had a message for both rulers and ruled. The election sermons of Puritan divines in colonial New England were based on that assumption. "It is better," John Cotton of Massachusetts declared, "that the commonwealth be fashioned to the setting forth of God's house, which is his church, than to accommodate the church to the civil state." And, as one scholar has commented on Cotton's statement, "every Puritan would have agreed." One of the few not to agree was Rhode Island's founder, Roger Williams, who denied the continuity between biblical "government," either in the kingdom of Israel or in the kingdom of God proclaimed by Jesus, and the "rule of the saints" claimed by Puritanism. In many ways, it was Abraham Lincoln who, during the conflict over slavery, discovered the fallacy in the traditional assumption. And the decisive authority for this discovery was, also according to Lincoln, the person of Jesus as the Mirror of the Eternal, who thus provided, in two traditions that could be traced to the Reformation, both the justification of "theocracy" and its most telling refutation.

Religious liberty, it has been said, was the product of the Reformation, but not of the Reformers, each of whom in one way or another took it to be the commandment of Christ to repress those who believed otherwise. Yet the religious conflicts brought about by the Reformation strongly contributed to the growing sense—to which Roger Williams gave concrete legal form in Rhode Island—that there was a moral obligation to respect the individual conscience (in the name of which the Reformers spoke and acted) even when it disagreed with the Reformers.

Onward, Christian soldiers,
Marching as to war,
With the cross of Jesus
Going on before.
—*Sabine Baring-Gould*
    Processional

14 ✢ The Prince of Peace

One of the *Names of Christ* to which Luis de León devoted his treatise under
that title was "Prince of Peace," from Isaiah 9:6: "To us a Child is born, to us a
Son is given; . . . and his name will be called . . . Prince of Peace." There was reason enough in the age of the Reformation, which was also the age of the Wars
of Religion, to emphasize that Jesus, as Prince of Peace, called on his followers
to seek the ways of peace and not of war. One of the last Reformation leaders,
John Amos Comenius, who with his Moravian church and nation suffered in
the Thirty Years' War, denounced those who "have gathered spears, swords,
wheels, halters, crosses, flames, and headsmen, so making them rather to be
feared than loved. Is this what was taught by the best of Teachers? Does this
proceed from the teachings of Him who commended to His followers nought

In August 1941, Franklin Delano Roosevelt, president of the United States, and Winston Spencer Churchill, prime minister of Great Britain, met at sea to formulate what came to be called the Atlantic Charter. Speaking on 24 August after his return to London, Churchill reported that at the services on shipboard "we sang 'Onward Christian Soldiers.' And indeed I felt that this was no vain presumption, but that we had the right to feel that we were serving a cause for the sake of which a trumpet has sounded from on high."

but love, and affection, and mutual help?" The Reformation answered Comenius's question of what the person and teaching of Jesus meant for the problem of war with a spectrum of theories, which may be organized in the standard threefold typology of teachings about "Jesus and war": the doctrine of just war, the theory of crusade, and the ideology of Christian pacifism.

Luther's defense of just war as what the best of Teachers had taught was addressed to the question "whether the Christian faith, by which we are accounted righteous before God, is compatible with being a soldier, going to war, stabbing and killing, robbing and burning, as military law requires us to do to our enemies in wartime? Is this work sinful or unjust? Should it give us a bad conscience before God? Must a Christian only do good and love, and kill no one, nor do anyone any harm?" The distinction between the spiritual kingdom of Christ and the earthly kingdom of this world provided Luther with a framework to resolve the contradiction between the absolute love-ethic of Jesus and the concrete duties of political life and military service. Absolute love was incumbent on the follower of Jesus as a person, but it was not to be the norm for the duties of such a follower's public office.

The nature of both kingdoms was, according to Luther, set forth in the words of Jesus to Pontius Pilate: "My kingship is not of this world; if my kingship were of this world, my servants would fight" (John 18:36). On one hand, Christ did not want to interfere with the kingdoms of this world and their structures, since his kingship belonged to another order; military action, therefore, was not an appropriate means of defending the kingdom of Christ. But Christ meant as well "that war was not wrong" in and of itself, since Jesus was saying, on the other hand, that in the kingdoms that did belong to this world it was appropriate for his "servants" as citizens to fight. Similarly, as both Calvin and Luther argued, John the Baptist did not tell the soldiers who asked, "And we, what shall we do?" that it was their duty, in the name of love, to renounce their sinful office of fighting and killing; he only "said to them, 'Rob no one by violence or by false accusation, and be content with your wages'" (Luke 3:14). Thus "he praised the military profession, but at the same time he forbade its abuse. Now the abuse does not affect the office." The coming of Christ meant, therefore, the introduction of the radically new imperative of suffering love; but that imperative was not addressed to Pilate and other Roman officers, nor to soldiers, pagan or Christian, who were to go on obeying the imperatives of their public office.

An even more skillful exegesis enabled Luther to cope with another saying of Jesus that appeared to be applying the radical love ethic to prohibit the use of force by his disciples. When Peter sought to protect Jesus by striking one of his captors with a sword, Jesus

When Peter drew a sword to defend Jesus against his captors, Jesus commanded him, "Put your sword back" (Matt. 26:52). In the event, not only was Jesus' authority invoked to justify the use of the sword to preserve public order, but in his name the armies of Europe went forth on Crusade to defend the faith and to wrest the Holy Land from the control of the Muslim "infidels." Their generals included Frederick Barbarossa and Richard Lion-Heart, but they believed that Christ himself was their supreme military commander.

Although Jesus had taught by the seaside and on at least one occasion (Mark 4:35–41) proved himself more seaworthy than the experienced sailors and fishermen among his disciples, it remained for later generations to represent him as patron of fighting ships and men-of-war, as on this Elizabethan galleon, decorated "with the cross of Jesus going on before."

reproved him, "Put your sword back into its place; for all who take the sword will perish by the sword" (Matt. 26:52). Those words did seem to forbid the use of the sword, also adding the threat that such use would ultimately bring a similar violence upon the perpetrator. Thus the commandment of Jesus was an extension of the words (Rom. 12:19): "Beloved, never avenge yourselves, but leave it to the wrath of God; for it is written (Deut. 32:35), 'Vengeance is mine, I will repay, says the Lord.'" But according to Luther, the warning of Jesus really meant that "the sword" was "a godly estate," through which that vengeance which was God's sole prerogative would be carried out: "All who take the sword [as private persons rather than in the faithful execution of a public office] will perish by the sword," a sword to be wielded by the incumbents of a public office—be they executioners or soldiers, pagans or Christians.

As for the prohibition of Jesus (Matt. 7:1), "Judge not," it, too, was to be taken in the light of the declaration, "Vengeance is mine." Rather than prohibiting war and the use of force, the imperative of Jesus made it incumbent upon his followers to respect established political order, even when rulers were unjust and oppressive. For "if this king keeps neither God's law nor the law of the land, ought you to attack him, judge him, and take vengeance on him?" That was precisely what Jesus was forbidding. Luther read the ethic of Jesus, therefore, as a condemnation of revolution, not of war; for revolution was by definition an act of injustice, but war could be an instrument of justice. Thus the mainstream of the Reformation attached itself to the just war tradition of Augustine and Thomas Aquinas.

Augustine had denounced Roman militarism, with its glorification of armed violence, and had used war as evidence that human beings could be more bloodthirsty than wild animals. Nevertheless, he had, somewhat reluctantly, conceded that "just wars" were made necessary by human wrongdoing; yet even then, he added, one must "lament the necessity of just wars," not glory in them. "Peace should be the object of your desire," Augustine warned the Christian governor of the province of Africa, and therefore "war should be waged only as a necessity, and waged only that God may by it deliver men from the emergency and preserve them in peace." From this it followed that "even in waging war" a follower of Christ was to "cherish the spirit of a peacemaker," as Jesus had said (Matt. 5:9). Quoting many of these same sayings, Thomas Aquinas proceeded from the distinction between private person and public office. There were three conditions necessary to make a war just: the one waging it must have the authority to do so; there must be a "just cause"; and the war must be carried on with the "right intention" of advancing the good and achieving the peace. Sayings of Jesus such as "Do not resist one who is evil" (Matt. 5:39) were indeed the ultimate authority for the follower of Jesus as a private person; "nevertheless, it is sometimes necessary for the common good for a man to act otherwise" in the execution of a public office. Later Thomists would add a fourth condition

Few figures in history have more paradoxically but more successfully combined the fighting heart of the warrior with a mystical devotion to Christ and to his Mother than Joan of Arc, "the maid of Orleans," who rallied the armies of France under a banner with the inscription "Jesus, Maria" in 1429. The paradox continued when Joan was burned at the stake for heresy in 1431— and canonized as a saint in 1920! Anna Hyatt Huntington's powerful statue captures both motifs.

The radical wing of the Protestant Reformation in the sixteenth century included both Christian pacifists and Christian militants. Among the latter, Thomas Münzer found in the sayings of "the gentle Son of God" not only "Put your sword back" (Matt. 26:52) but "I have not come to bring peace, but a sword" (Matt. 10:34). Carrying out what he believed to be the implications of Christ's command, Münzer led a Christian revolution in the Peasants' War and died for the cause in 1525, during the Battle of Mühlhausen, depicted here.

(and one that has become important in discussion of nuclear war): that the war be carried on "*debito modo,* with appropriate [and thus appropriately limited] means."

There was, however, one aspect of the treatment of war in medieval theology on which Luther broke radically with his predecessors: the Crusade, the tradition of "Christian soldiers" who, as such, were "marching as to war." As a solution for the moral ambiguity of war that went beyond the tragic necessity implied in the Augustinian idea of just war, the Crusade imprinted the sacred sign of the cross of Jesus on the cause of "Holy Peace and Holy War." "To take the cross" meant to go off to war against Islam in Palestine, wearing a cross of red cloth on the shoulder of one's outer garment. Pope Urban II seems to have described the death of Crusaders in battle as a kind of participation in the sufferings and death of Christ. In the event, however, as the historian of the Crusades Steven Runciman has put it, this "Crusading fervour" in the name of Jesus "always provided an excuse for killing God's enemies" and led to pogroms against Jews and the sack of Christian Constantinople—all of these being flagrant negations of the teachings of the very One whose cross they bore.

By the Reformation period, the Crusade to free the Holy Land from the infidel had fallen into virtual oblivion, for the Turks had become a clear and present danger to Christian Europe itself, at the very time that the Reformation seemed to be dividing the Christian forces. The coincidence of the two threats was the occasion for the convoking of the diet of the Holy Roman Empire at Augsburg in 1530, where the Augsburg Confession presented the case for the Lutheran Reformation, making it the official position of the Reformation party that Charles V, "His Imperial Majesty, may in salutary and godly fashion imitate the example of David in making war on the Turk." The reason given for approving war against the Turk was not the Crusade ideal of a holy war but the principle that the "incumbent of a royal office" had the right, indeed the obligation, of "the defense and protection of [his] subjects." The mainstream of the Reformation rejected the Crusade ideal but insisted on the just war theory: it was legitimate on account of the Jesus who acknowledged that Pontius Pilate possessed an authority from God (John 19:11), not the Jesus whose crucifixion under Pontius Pilate gave authority to his church (Matt. 28:19–20).

The most broadly disseminated portrait of Jesus ever painted, in many hundreds of millions of copies, was Warner Sallman's Head of Christ, *shown earlier as the* Bridegroom of the Soul. *During World War II not only that image but the more explicitly martial* Christmas Story *of 1942 made Christ the solace and inspiration of American soldiers, even though, as Abraham Lincoln had observed ironically about an earlier war, both sides "read the same Bible, and pray to the same God; and each invokes his aid against the other."*

Together with his fellow believers, the last bishop of the Unity of Bohemian Brethren, John Amos Comenius (Komenský)—whose statue, a gift from the Czech people, dominates the campus of Moravian College in Bethlehem, Pennsylvania—was driven from his homeland after the Battle of White Mountain in 1620. Viewing the spectacle of Christian Europe destroying itself in the Thirty Years' War, and doing so in the name of Christ, he asked: "Is this what was taught by the best of Teachers?"

The nearest analogue to the Crusade ideal in the Reformation era came from a leader of the Radical Reformation, Thomas Münzer. He was convinced that "Christ the Son of God and his apostles" had established a pure faith but that it had been corrupted immediately thereafter. That precious Stone, Jesus Christ, was "about to fall and strike these schemes . . . and dash them to the ground." For Jesus had warned: "Do not think that I have come to bring peace on earth; I have not come to bring peace, but a sword" (Matt. 10:34). He had, moreover, "commanded in deep gravity, saying: 'Take these enemies of mine and strangle them before my very eyes' (Luke 19:27)." And why did the Prince of Peace, whom Münzer himself here called "the gentle Son of God," issue such a bloodthirsty command? "Ah, because they ruin Christ's government for him. . . . Now if you want to be true governors, you must begin government at the roots, and, as Christ commanded, drive his enemies from the elect." The summons of Jesus was a call for Christian revolution, a new kind of holy war. Münzer was captured and beheaded the following year; but his spirit would live on, through the radical political apocalypticism of the Fifth Monarchy Men, who emerged from English Puritanism in the seventeenth century, and then through the "liberation theology" of some twentieth-century Christians.

Münzer's theology of holy war ended in the debacle of the Peasants' War; Luther's theory of just war ended in the catastrophe of the Thirty Years' War. Neither holy war nor just war, moreover, constituted a new answer to the dilemma of Jesus and war, as formulated by Comenius: "Is this what was taught by the best of Teachers?" The only truly new answer (which, they insisted, was actually very old) came first from Erasmus, then from

PEACEABLE KINGDOM

The vision of Jesus Christ as Prince of Peace, as articulated by Quaker thinkers like William Penn and Quaker artists like Edward Hicks, saw him as the pacifier of all ancient enmities—between one nation and another, between races, and even between humanity and its fellow creatures on earth, "because the creation itself will be set free from its bondage to decay and obtain the glorious liberty of the children of God" (Rom. 8:21).

certain Anabaptists, Quakers, and other peace groups of the Radical Reformation. Although they often invoked arguments from reason and from universal human morality in their attacks on war, it was christology—a christology of life rather than principally a christology of doctrine—that constituted the heart of their argument. The foundation of that argument was the definition of the essence of Christianity as discipleship. "In the ninth chapter of Matthew," the Anabaptists declared, "Christ came to Matthew the tax collector and said to him, 'Follow me' (Matt. 9:9)." Reviving the New Testament call for a drastic break with the past as the condition for authentic discipleship, they announced "the way of the cross," on which the disciple followed Jesus into death and through death into life. Some of the most profoundly stirring documents to come out of the Reformation are the accounts of the martyrdom of Anabaptists, who "marched to the scaffold as though they were going to a dance" because they saw this as an opportunity to participate in the death and resurrection of Jesus.

The evangelical Anabaptists believed themselves to be summoned to a yielded life of total dependence on God, the kind of life Christ himself had lived. They were not to try to reshape the external world and the civil order into a Christian society in conformity with

Whatever the life and teachings of Jesus may have implied to Christian pacifists or Christian crusaders for the issues of peace and war, the implications of his death were clearer for both. "In Flanders' fields," the World War I poet John McCrae wrote, "the crosses, row on row" identified the victims of war with Christ the Eternal Victim on his cross. So it is on countless other military burial grounds, with crosses as far as the eye can see.

the will of Jesus but to become the "little flock" of Jesus (Luke 12:32). They called on the true disciples of Jesus the Prince of Peace to separate themselves drastically from the world. It was into the context of that image of Jesus that the pacifist Anabaptists put their interpretation of war and of the use of force, succinctly stated in the Schleitheim Confession of 1527: "We are agreed as follows concerning the sword: The sword is ordained of God outside the perfection of Christ. It punishes and puts to death the wicked, and guards and protects the good. . . . In the perfection of Christ, however, only the ban is used for a warning and for the excommunication of the one who has sinned, without putting the flesh to death." Echoing the words of the New Testament, the Anabaptists acknowledged that God had instituted government, which "does not bear the sword in vain" (Rom. 13:1–4). They were intent not on overthrowing the governing authorities but on supporting them. What they opposed was the idea that the followers of Christ could themselves be magistrates and wield the sword.

A similar concept of "the perfection of Christ" provided the next stage in the history of Christian pacifism. Through the Scottish Quaker Robert Barclay, the Society of Friends worked out a theological formulation of the case against Christian participation in war. For "the present magistrates of the Christian world," war was not "altogether unlawful," for they were still "far from the perfection of the Christian religion." But those who had reached this perfection had been led by the Spirit of Christ to see the fundamental inconsistency between warfare and "the law of Christ." True obedience to the law of Christ demanded of the Quakers that they not wage war but "suffer ourselves to be spoiled, taken, imprisoned, banished, beaten, and evilly entreated, without any resistance, placing our trust only in GOD, that he may defend us, and lead us by the way of the cross unto his kingdom."

It is noteworthy that several of those who attacked the traditional use of the teachings of Jesus to justify war were at the same time carrying on a vigorous campaign against the traditional dogmas about the person of Jesus Christ. And yet—the copies of the Gospels being read by both sides contained a parable of Jesus that contrasted saying the right thing and doing the right thing as follows: "What do you think? A man had two sons; and he went to the first and said, 'Son, go and work in the vineyard today.' And he answered, 'I will not'; but afterward he repented and went. And he went to the second and said the same; and he answered, 'I go, sir,' but did not go. Which of the two did the will of his father?" (Matt. 21:28–31).

What if men take to following where he leads,
Weary of mumbling Athanasian creeds?
—*Roden Noël,* The Red Flag

15 ✦ The Teacher of Common Sense

During the Age of Reason the orthodox Christian image of Jesus Christ came in for severe attack and drastic revision. The best-known revision was what Albert Schweitzer called "the quest of the Historical Jesus," but that quest was made possible, and necessary, by the Enlightenment's dethronement of the Cosmic Christ.

In 1730 there appeared in London the first volume of *Christianity as Old as the Creation, or, The Gospel, a Republication of the Religion of Nature* by Matthew Tindal, an effort to defend the gospel by equating its essence with reason and natural religion and by identifying Jesus as the Teacher of Common Sense. Tindal argued that a new understanding of Jesus had become necessary because miracles had disappeared as a proof for the uniqueness of his person

and the validity of his message. Throughout most of the history of Christianity, the historical credibility of the miracle stories was based on the theological doctrine of the divine nature of Jesus, which was in turn validated by the presumed scientific and philosophical possibility of miracles. That argument in a circle broke down in several places—scientific-philosophical, historical, and theological—but not all at the same time. We must look at each of them in turn, and at the implications of each for the image of Jesus.

Although the perception of Jesus as Logos and Cosmic Christ is credited as being one

Without intending in any way to detract from the uniqueness of Christ or to deny Catholic teaching about him, Caravaggio gave Jesus the appearance of an ordinary man among ordinary men, even in one of the most luminous of his appearances after the resurrection, the supper at Emmaus, where his disciples "recognized him" when "he took the bread and blessed it, and broke it, and gave it to them" (Luke 24:30–31).

of the philosophical sources of modern scientific thought, the scientific thought of the seventeenth and eighteenth centuries gradually eroded it. Isaac Newton declared his conviction, as an article of sound natural philosophy, that "this most beautiful system of the sun, planets, and comets" was not to be attributed to some "blind metaphysical necessity" but "could only proceed from the counsel and dominion of an intelligent and powerful Being," who governed all things, "not as the soul of the world, but as Lord over all" and in that sense transcendent. There was "nothing of contradiction" in acknowledging that as the First Cause, God could "vary the laws of Nature" (thus apparently allowing for the miraculous) and yet at the same time in assuming that the world "once formed . . . may continue by those laws for many ages" (thus apparently precluding the miraculous). Newton accepted the miracle stories as trustworthy, but he rejected the traditional doctrine of the person of Christ as incompatible both with reason and with Scripture.

It remained only to rule the miracles themselves out of court as inadmissible evidence. "There is not to be found in all history," the Scottish philosopher David Hume asserted, "any miracle attested by a sufficient number of men, of such unquestioned good-sense, education, and learning, as to secure us against all delusion in themselves." Asserting that not reason but faith was the foundation of "our most holy religion," he concluded, perhaps disingenuously, with the argument that faith was itself the greatest—indeed the only—miracle. For, as Goethe was to have Faust say, "Miracle is faith's most cherished child," rather than the other way around. In such a context the miracles of Jesus had lost all power to prove who he was.

Miracle was an issue not only for science but also for history. In his examination of five historical causes for the victory of Christianity in the Roman empire, the English historian Edward Gibbon used the issue of miracles to describe how thoroughly "credulity" and "fanaticism" had prevailed in the Christian movement of the first three centuries. "The duty of an historian," he observed, a bit archly, "does not call upon him to interpose his private judgment in this nice and important controversy" over whether miracles had continued after the apostolic age. And, even more coyly, Gibbon closed the chapter with a consideration also of the miracles of the apostolic age, above all the miracles performed by Jesus himself. "How shall we excuse the supine inattention of the Pagan and philosophic world to those evidences which were presented by the hand of Omnipotence, not to their reason, but to their senses?" Gibbon asked. For, he continued, "during the age of Christ, of his apostles, and of their first disciples, the doctrine which they preached was confirmed by innumerable prodigies. . . . The Laws of nature were frequently suspended for the benefit of the church." Then, focusing on the most spectacular miracle of all, he facetiously accused the classical writers of having "omitted to mention the greatest phenomenon to which the mortal eye has been witness since the creation of the globe . . . , the praeternatural darkness of the Passion," when the sun was obscured for three hours on Good Friday while Jesus hung on the cross.

In the same spirit Gibbon forbore to list the commanding moral and religious authority of the figure of Jesus Christ as one of his five "secondary causes of the rapid growth of the Christian church" but cited, as "an obvious but satisfying answer" to the whole question, that the triumph of Christianity (or, as he called it later, the "triumph of barbarism and religion") "was owing to the convincing evidence of the doctrine itself, and to the ruling providence of its great Author." Consideration of that answer, however, lay beyond "the duty of an historian." Instead, he subjected early Christianity to a searching, and in many ways devastating, historical analysis. But it was only in connection with the theological controversies over the person and the natures of Christ that he said anything significant about the life of Jesus at all, and even then he disposed of it in one paragraph: "The familiar companions of Jesus of Nazareth conversed with their friend and countryman, who, in all the actions of rational and animal life, appeared of the same

Originally invoked by the Greek apologists for Christianity in the second and third centuries, the parallel between Jesus and Socrates commended itself for quite different reasons to the rationalists of the Enlightenment. The Death of Socrates *by Charles-Alphonse Dufresnoy from 1787 carries out the parallel, even to the point of showing the friends of Socrates in an attitude that might have been as suitable for a painting of the twelve disciples at their last evening with Jesus before his death.*

species with themselves. His progress from infancy to youth and manhood was marked by a regular increase in stature and wisdom; and, after a painful agony of mind and body, he expired on the cross. He lived and died for the service of mankind; . . . the tears which he shed over his friend and country may be esteemed the purest evidence of his humanity."

In 1778, the German man of letters Gotthold Ephraim Lessing published an anonymous treatise entitled *Concerning the Intention of Jesus and His Teaching,* which set off a debate over the authentic message and purpose of Jesus that has continued now for more than two centuries and shows no sign of relenting. Its author was Hermann Samuel Reimarus. He insisted that it was not to miracles, which were "unworthy of notice," or to the disclosure of so-called mysteries that the success of Jesus and his message was to be attributed, but to purely natural causes, "a reason which operates and has operated at all times so naturally, that we need no miracle to make everything comprehensible and clear. That is the real mighty wind (Acts 2:2) that so quickly wafted all the people together. This is the true original language that performs the miracles." A century later, the radical biblical critic David Friedrich Strauss's *Life of Jesus* again focused attention on Reimarus in defense of the concept of "myth" as a means of finding the elusive figure behind the Gospel

Thomas Jefferson, third president of the United States, seems to have been interested in everything from dinosaur bones to fine cuisine. But he had a particular interest in a "purified Christianity" as a basis for life and morality in the new Republic. To achieve such a purification, he twice put his hand to editing the Gospels in order to separate "the diamond from the dung hill," first in The Philosophy of Jesus of Nazareth *in 1804 (while he was still in the White House) and then in* The Life and Morals of Jesus of Nazareth *in 1828 or so.*

The

Life and Morals

of

Jesus of Nazareth

Extracted textually

from the Gospels

in

Greek, Latin

French & English.

accounts. It was translated into English (anonymously) by a scholarly young English-woman named Mary Ann Evans, better known by her later nom de plume of George Eliot. As her biographer notes of her translation of Strauss, "Few books of the nineteenth century have had a profounder influence on religious thought in England."

From this time on, the quest of the Historical Jesus became the vocation also of intellectuals other than theologians. In a search for new ways of understanding reality, validating morality, and organizing society, now that the old orthodoxy had been discredited, these intellectuals undertook to reinterpret the major classics of Western culture in a manner that would make their abiding message available to a new age. If metaphysical unity with God in the Trinity and miraculous revelation from on high no longer constituted credentials for the message of Jesus, the harmony between his message and the best of human wisdom everywhere could.

The parallels between Socrates and Jesus were especially intriguing. Both Socrates and Jesus were outstanding teachers; both urged and practiced great simplicity of life; both were regarded as traitors to the religion of their community; neither wrote anything; both of them were executed; and both have become the subject of traditions that are difficult or impossible to harmonize. Yet the study of the parallel went even beyond those striking similarities. For the thinkers of the Enlightenment took Socrates as evidence for the presence, beyond the limits of alleged biblical revelation, of a wisdom and moral power that must have come from the same God whom Jesus called Father. If the Logos

was "the true light that enlightens every man" (John 1:9), whether Jew or Greek, Christian or heathen, Socrates made it extremely difficult to restrict the revealing activity of God— perhaps even the saving activity of God—to the history of Israel and the church. And if the true God had spoken and acted through Socrates, that meant that divine truth was universal. If it was universal, then both Socrates and Jesus must themselves have taught that it was. Joseph Priestley, scientist and scholar, took up the question of disentangling the Historical Jesus from the sources in his *Corruptions of Christianity* and his *Harmony of the Gospels*. In *Socrates and Jesus Compared* he strove to do justice to the philosophical greatness and moral stature of Socrates but came down on the side of the essential superiority of Jesus. Jesus was no longer the Cosmic Christ or the Second Person of the Trinity, but he was a divinely inspired teacher in a way that even Socrates was not.

Priestley's biblical scholarship profoundly influenced one man who was certainly the most eminent of the many participants in the quest of the Historical Jesus: Thomas Jefferson, third president of the United States, who was convinced, as the historian Daniel Boorstin has noted, that a "purified Christianity could promote moral health in the actual setting of eighteenth-century America." In Jefferson's judgment, doctrines like the Trinity were not needed to account for Jesus of Nazareth, who was "a man, of illegitimate birth, of a benevolent heart, enthusiastic mind, who set out without pretensions of divinity, ended in believing them, and was punished capitally for sedition by being gibbeted according to the Roman law." Nor was it enough simply to reject the dogmatic and liturgical tradition of orthodox Christianity or to restore the message of the Bible. Jefferson was convinced that the authentic message of Jesus was not to be equated with the total content of the Gospels and that therefore it was necessary to extract that message from the texts. Out of that conviction came two attempts at what he called "abstracting what is really his from the rubbish in which it is buried, easily distinguished by it's lustre from the dross of his biographers, and as separable from that as the diamond from the dung hill."

In February 1804, working in the White House—as he admitted later, "too hastily"—he completed the task in "2. or 3. nights only at Washington, after getting thro' the evening task of reading the letters and papers of the day." The outcome bore the title *The Philosophy of Jesus of Nazareth,* containing those sayings in the Gospels that Jefferson recognized to be authentic. Probably in the summer of 1820, Jefferson completed work on a much more ambitious compilation, *The Life and Morals of Jesus of Nazareth Extracted Textually from the Gospels in Greek, Latin, French, and English.* More revealing in many ways than what is included is what is omitted. Both the beginning and the end of the Gospel story have disappeared. The prologue of the Gospel of John is gone, and so are the accounts of the annunciation, the virgin birth, and the appearance of the angels to the shepherds. The account closes with a conflation of the first half of John 19:42 with the second half of Matthew 27:60: "There laid they Jesus and rolled a great stone to the door of the sepulchre, and departed." There is no mention of the resurrection. In *The Philosophy of Jesus,* Luke 2:40 had appeared in full, "And the child grew, and waxed strong in spirit, filled with wisdom; and the grace of God was upon him." But in *The Life and Morals of Jesus of Nazareth,* Jefferson took the trouble to expunge, in all four languages, the final eight words. As the editor of Jefferson's version of the Gospel puts its, rather gently but no less effectively, "Although many distinguished biblical scholars have been daunted by the challenge of disentangling the many layers of the New Testament, the rationalistic Jefferson was supremely confident of his ability to differentiate between the true and the false precepts of Jesus."

The Jesus who emerged was the Teacher of Common Sense, or, in Jefferson's words, "the greatest of all the Reformers of the depraved religion of his own country"—that "depraved religion" being, of course, Judaism. The content of his message was a morality of absolute love and service, which did not depend either upon the dogma of his divinity or even upon the claim that he had a unique inspiration from God but authenticated itself to his hearers by its intrinsic worth. Many of these elements of the Enlightenment image of Jesus are tersely summarized in the letter that Jefferson's colleague, Benjamin Franklin, wrote a few weeks before his death to theologian and president of Yale College Ezra Stiles: "As to Jesus of Nazareth, my opinion of whom you particularly desire, I think the system of morals and religion, as he left them to us, the best the world ever saw or is likely to see; but I apprehend it has received various corrupting changes, and I have, with most of the present dissenters in England, some doubts as to his divinity, tho' it is a question I do not dogmatize upon, having never studied it, and think it needless to busy myself with it now, when I expect soon an opportunity of knowing the truth with less trouble. I see no harm, however, in its being believed, if that belief has the good consequence, as probably it has, of making his doctrines more respected and better observed." For Franklin and Jefferson, that message of common sense was enough, and Franklin's *Poor Richard's Almanack* can be read as a compilation of it. But for many others, it was either too much or too little— or perhaps both.

Self, that no alien knows!
Self, far diffused as Fancy's wing can travel!
Self, spreading still! Oblivious of its own,
Yet all of all possessing! This is Faith!
This the Messiah's destined victory!
—Samuel Taylor Coleridge
Religious Musings

16 ❖ The Poet of the Spirit

Much of nineteenth-century thought and literature leveled the charge against its predecessors of the eighteenth century that by reducing mystery to reason and by flattening transcendence into common sense, the rationalism of the Enlightenment had dethroned superstition only to enthrone banality. What the nineteenth century substituted for such rationalism was the Romantic vision, which René Wellek called the "attempt, apparently doomed to failure and abandoned by our time, to identify subject and object, to reconcile man and nature, consciousness and unconsciousness by poetry which is 'the first and last of all knowledge.'" Wellek was defining Romanticism, which for our purposes we may characterize as the effort of nineteenth-century thinkers to go beyond the quest of the Historical Jesus to a Jesus who could be called the Poet

Ralph Waldo Emerson began as a Unitarian minister. Although he found even that affiliation too constricting and resigned his ordination, he became, on the lecture circuit and by his books, "the Sage of Concord"—in fact, the sage of New England and of much of the English-speaking world. His shocking "Address" to the Harvard Divinity School in 1838 identified Jesus Christ as having "belonged to the true race of the prophets. . . . One man was true to what is in you and me. He saw that God incarnates himself in man, and evermore goes forth anew to take possession of his World."

"The tale of [Christ's] life will cause endless tears," wrote the French Romantic Joseph Ernest Renan, and each of the major events of the tale (arranged here chronologically) came to express Romantic sensibilities and to evoke such tears. In that tale, the imagery and folklore traditionally surrounding the Nativity of Christ had already moved Gerrit van Honthorst, who thanks to Caravaggio was "a Romantic painter before the age of Romanticism," to make the Mother so radiant and the Christ Child so appealing (opposite page) that the response to them must be universal.

of the Spirit, or, in words that Coleridge wrote on Christmas Eve 1794, to find "faith" and "the Messiah's destined victory" in the vindication of "Self, that no alien knows!"

Five years later, as if to announce the end of the eighteenth century, the leading German interpreter of this Romantic version of faith in Christ, Friedrich Schleiermacher, translator of Plato into German, issued his *On Religion: Speeches to Its Cultured Despisers*. He went on, in 1806, to publish a kind of Platonic dialogue about Christ entitled *Christmas Eve Celebration* and, in 1819, to become "the first person to lecture publicly on the topic of the life of Jesus." Among English writers, probably the most profound as well as the most important of the transmitters of German Romanticism was Coleridge, who was in turn a major force in the intellectual and spiritual development of Ralph Waldo Emerson, probably the most influential thinker in nineteenth-century America. Each of these three was a highly individual spokesman for the literary and philosophical spirit of Romanticism, and sought the incarnation of that spirit in the person of Jesus.

Like the rationalists, they found it impossible to accept the miracles of Jesus as literal historical truth, but they endeavored to incorporate them into a more comprehensive world view. As Coleridge put it, "What we now consider as miracles in opposition to ordinary experience" would, with further insight, be seen "with a yet higher devotion as harmonious parts of one great complex miracle, when the antithesis between experience and belief would itself be taken up into [the] unity of intuitive reason." Both the attack on the

notion of miracles and the theological defense had missed the point; for on both sides, in Emerson's phrase, "the savant becomes unpoetic," through the failure to realize "that a guess is often more fruitful than an indisputable affirmation, and that a dream may let us deeper into the secret of nature than a hundred concerted experiments."

In this search for a "unity of intuitive reason" that would go beyond the antitheses between nature and miracle or between experience and belief, Jesus was, they recognized, the crucial problem and, they also believed, the source for its solution. Schleiermacher discarded as not very helpful "the contrast between the supernatural and the natural that we include in the term 'miracle' on the basis of scholastic terminology." Miracles were important as a "sign" and "mighty work," in which not the suspension of the laws of nature but the "significance" was the primary component. Confronted by the Gospel accounts of

*In the three temptations that the
Evil One addressed to Jesus in the
wilderness (Matt. 4:1–11)—to live
by bread alone without the word of
God, to tempt God by hurling
himself over a precipice, and to gain
power and glory by compromising
with the devil—nineteenth-century
Russians from Dostoyevsky to
Kramskoy found a summary of
the fundamental questions
of life and faith.*

the miracles, therefore, the biographer of Jesus had to relate them to the central themes of
his life and work: "The more the deed can be understood as a moral act on the part of
Christ and the more we can establish a comparison between Christ's way of accomplish-
ing a given result and that employed by other people, the more we can comprehend the
acts as genuine constituents of the life of Jesus. The less we can understand them as moral
acts on Christ's part and the less at the same time we can discover analogies, the less we
shall be able to form a definite idea of the account and understand the facts on which it is
based."

The central content of the biography of Jesus, in Schleiermacher's *Life,* was the "development" in him of a "God-consciousness" that was, in comparison with the God-consciousness of others, "perfect" and therefore unique in degree, but not fundamentally different in kind. What was distinctive about Jesus was neither "the purity of his moral
teaching" nor even "the individuality of his character, the close union of high power with
touching gentleness," both of which were present in every great religious teacher. But "the
truly divine element is the glorious clearness to which the great idea he came to exhibit

attained in his soul": namely, "that all that is finite requires a higher mediation to be in accord with the Deity, and that for man under the power of the finite and the particular, and too ready to imagine the divine itself in this form, salvation is only to be found in redemption."

Because such "God-consciousness" and divine inspiration had been manifested with special force in artists and poets, the aesthetic experience provided the most appropriate categories for interpreting Jesus. In his early work on the life and teachings of Jesus, *The Spirit of Christianity and Its Fate,* Hegel defined "truth" as "beauty intellectually represented," and he therefore saw "the spirit of Jesus" as "a spirit raised above morality." Jesus had, of course, been an inspiration to artists, poets, and musicians since the beginnings of Christianity. What sets much of the nineteenth century apart from that universal tradition is the effort to make this poetic and artistic understanding of him supersede the dogmatic, moral, and even historical understandings. William Blake's unfinished poem *The Everlasting Gospel* resembled other attempts of the time: Blake's Jesus, as the embodiment of what he calls the "poetic," denounced in his words, and violated in his deeds, the conventionalities of gentle and genteel religion. In Blake's case, moreover, the poetic and artistic understanding of Jesus takes on special meaning, because Blake created portraits of Jesus in which the antithesis between nature and supernature is transcended.

Almost an exact contemporary of Cardinal Newman and of Tennyson, the Scottish painter William Dyce was a scholar and professor of fine arts at King's College, London. In his portrayal of Jesus, as in his more secular works, he showed the benefits he had gained from his study of earlier artistic creations.

It was the belief of many Romantic poets and thinkers that, in Wordsworth's phrase, children come into the world "trailing clouds of glory." This sentiment was easily adapted to the spirit, naive and profound at the same time, of the words of Jesus in Mark 10:14, "Let the children come to me, do not hinder them; for to such belongs the kingdom of God."

It was, the Romantics argued, hasty and superficial to conclude from the scientific discovery of the natural world that now all mystery had been exorcised from it. If the mystery of faith did not make sense to the eighteenth century, then perhaps the mystery of beauty could. For, as Emerson said, "The ancient Greeks called the world *kosmos,* beauty. Such is the constitution of all things, or such the plastic power of the human eye, that the primary forms, as the sky, the mountain, the tree, the animal, give us a delight *in and for themselves.*" He sought to "look upon Nature with the eye of the Artist," for in that way he could "learn from the great Artist whose blood beats in our veins, whose taste is upspringing in our own perception of beauty." The medieval *analogia entis,* the analogy of being between Creator and creature, had now become an aesthetic *analogia Naturae,* an analogy of Nature.

More even than in these thinkers, aestheticism shaped the presentation of the biography of Jesus published in 1863 by Emerson's French contemporary Ernest Renan. It was a celebration of what Renan called "the poetry of the soul—faith, liberty, virtue, devotion," as this had been voiced by Jesus, the Poet of the Spirit. "This sublime person," he said, "who every day still presides over the destiny of the world, we may call divine," not in the sense in which that word had been employed by orthodox dogma but because "his worship will constantly renew its youth, the tale of his life will cause endless tears, his sufferings will soften the best hearts." As a historian, Renan invoked the aesthetic mystery as an antidote to the ravages of a rationalistic historical skepticism. It was, he urged, necessary for the historian to understand how a faith "has charmed and satisfied the human conscience," but equally necessary not to believe it any longer, because "absolute faith is incompatible with sincere history." But he consoled himself with the belief that "to abstain from attaching one's self to any of the forms which captivate the adoration of men, is not to deprive ourselves of the enjoyment of that which is good and beautiful in them." So it was to be with Jesus.

Many efforts to cast the person of Jesus in such a mold came to grief on the moral question. Try though they did, these theologians of Romanticism could not connect their fundamental category of an aesthetic appreciation of Jesus to the prophetic earnestness that had been unmistakably present in his summons to discipleship. For Emerson, the crisis came in the conflict over slavery during the decades before the Civil War. He had attempted, in an essay of 1844 entitled "The Poet," to bring together the True, the Good, and the Beautiful. "The Universe," he said there, "has three children, born at one time." "Theologically," he continued, they had been called "the Father, the Spirit and the Son," but "we will call [them] here the Knower, the Doer and the Sayer." "These stand respectively," he explained, "for the love of truth, for the love of good, and for the love of beauty." "The three are equal," he added in an obvious allusion to a trinitarian dogma that he had rejected as a Unitarian even before he became a Transcendentalist. It was the task of the poet to be the sayer and the namer, and to represent beauty. In that task he stood in continuity with God. "For the world is not painted or adorned, but is from the beginning beautiful; and God has not made some beautiful things, but Beauty is the creator of the universe." As Jesus was the Poet of the Spirit, so now the poet was to be the new Second Person of the Trinity, through whom the Beauty that was the creator of the universe would shine through, manifesting its essential unity with Truth and Goodness. But at the end of the essay Emerson lamented: "I look in vain for the poet whom I describe. . . . Time and nature yield us many gifts, but not yet the timely man, the new religion, the reconciler, whom all things await."

In its concrete performance as an outlook on the past and as a method for understanding history, Romanticism demonstrated that it had an antenna more sensitive to the signals of tradition than the Rationalism that sought to lay exclusive claim to truly scientific history. It is difficult to see how our present awareness of the culture and thought of the Middle Ages could have developed as it did if it had not been for the pervasive force of Romanticism. In 1845, John Henry Newman, who is sometimes associated with Romanticism, published his *Essay on Development,* which has greatly influenced both the rediscovery and the recovery of tradition.

On graduation evening, Sunday, 15 July 1838, Ralph Waldo Emerson, at the invitation of the senior class of the Harvard Divinity School, delivered an address that scandalized New England and barred him from returning to Harvard for almost thirty years. In it he attacked "historical Christianity" for having "dwelt . . . with noxious exaggeration about the *person* of Jesus." Yet "the soul knows no persons." Instead of urging that "[you] live after the infinite Law that is in you, and in company with the infinite Beauty which heaven and earth reflect to you in all lovely forms," this Christianity demanded that "you must subordinate your nature to Christ's nature; you must accept our interpretations, and take his portrait as the vulgar draw it." That was a violation of the imperative to "every man to expand to the full circle of the universe," with "no preferences but those of spontaneous love." But it also violated the authentic portrait of Jesus. "His doctrine and memory" had suffered a grave "distortion" already in his own time, and even more in "the following ages," when "the figures of his rhetoric have usurped the place of his truth." The church could not tell the difference between prose and poetry, and those who professed to be his orthodox followers threatened their theological adversaries, saying, "This was Jehovah come down out of heaven. I will kill you, if you say he was a man." Preachers and theologians, Emerson said, "do not see that they make his gospel not glad, and shear him of the locks of beauty and the attributes of heaven."

How different was the true message of Jesus as Poet of the Spirit! "A true conversion, a true Christ, is now, as always, to be made by the reception of beautiful sentiments." Those beautiful sentiments were not confined to the Jesus of the Gospels, but they had achieved

For Romanticism, "the truly divine element" in Jesus was "the glorious clearness to which the great idea he came to exhibit attained in his soul," the idea "that all that is finite requires a higher mediation to be in accord with the Deity." The epitome of the Romantic conception of Jesus as Poet of the Spirit, Heinrich Hofmann's Jesus in the Garden of Gethsemane, *which was painted in Germany in 1890, was popular not only in books, devotional literature, and religious journals but in stained glass windows, murals, and altar paintings.*

If Romanticism was, in the definition of René Wellek, the attempt "to identify subject and object, to reconcile man and nature, consciousness and unconsciousness by poetry which is 'the first and last of all knowledge,'" Caspar David Friedrich's Cross in the Mountains *(opposite page), with its Romantic depiction of tree, sky, and mountain, makes Christ the crucified the one who poetically reconciles man and nature and who thus brings together subject and object, consciousness and unconsciousness.*

In William Blake's unfinished poem, The Everlasting Gospel, *Jesus was the embodiment of what he called the "poetic," just as he was in Blake's painting of the resurrection of Christ, in which the already otherworldly quality of Blake's other representations of the life of Jesus attains a transcendent and almost eerie radiance.*

their pinnacle there, because they were universal: "Jesus Christ belonged to the true race of the prophets. He saw with open eye the mystery of the soul. Drawn by its severe harmony, ravished with its beauty, he lived in it, and had his being there. Alone in all history he estimated the greatness of man. One man was true to what is in you and me. He saw that God incarnates himself in man, and evermore goes forth anew to take possession of his World. He said, in this jubilee of sublime emotion, 'I am divine. Through me, God acts; through me, speaks. Would you see God, see me; or see thee, when thou also thinkest as I now think.'" Therefore, Emerson went on to say, "it is the office of a true teacher to show us that God is, not was; that He speaketh, not spake." Otherwise, "the true Christianity—a faith like Christ's in the infinitude of men—is lost." He concluded by expressing this hope: "That supreme Beauty which ravished the souls of those Eastern men" of

the Bible "shall speak in the West also," showing "that the Ought, that Duty, is one thing with Science, with Beauty, and with Joy." Therefore, he urged the neophyte minister of Jesus Christ, "Yourself a newborn bard of the Holy Ghost, cast behind you all conformity, and acquaint men at first hand with Deity." For that was truly faithful to the person and message of Jesus, Poet of the Spirit.

But the poetic treatment of the person of Jesus could also move in quite another direction. In Dostoyevsky's *Crime and Punishment,* Raskolnikov demands that Sonia read to him the story of the resurrection of Lazarus. As she reads, it is as though she were

The "harlot with the heart of gold" was a cliché of Romantic fiction and drama, but Christian paintings and novels were able to give it a special turn by focusing on Mary Magdalene (opposite page), whom tradition (though not the New Testament) identified with the adulterous woman brought to Jesus for his judgment (John 8:3–11) and whom the New Testament did identify as the first one to whom the risen Christ appeared (John 19:11–18).

One achievement of Romanticism was a recovery of tradition, which often expressed itself as nostalgia for a golden age but which also cultivated a sensitivity to the past as a dimension of the present. By taking seriously both change and continuity in history, John Henry Newman's Essay on Development *of 1845 gave that sensitivity a new sophistication; and in a poem of 1833, "The Pillar of the Cloud," he identified Jesus Christ as the "Kindly Light" who alone could lead him "through th' encircling gloom" of both past and present to the future "morn," in which "those angel faces smile / Which I have loved long since, and lost awhile." Pope Leo XIII made him a cardinal in 1879, when he was nearly eighty.*

"making a public confession of faith." At first, her reading "passionately reproduced the doubt, the reproach and censure" of those who refused to accept Christ. But when she came to the miracle of the raising of Lazarus, she was "cold and trembling with ecstasy, as though she were seeing it before her very eyes." As the candle guttered, it cast its dying light on "the murderer and the harlot who had so strangely been reading together the holy book," a new Magdalene and a new Lazarus. And the result was that Raskolnikov knew he must confess to her his murder of the old pawnbroker. When he finally did so, Sonia told him what he must do: "Go at once, this very minute . . . kiss the earth which

The encounter between Raskolnikov and Sonia in Dostoyevsky's Crime and Punishment *had at its center the Gospel account of the miracle of the raising of Lazarus by Christ. As Sonia was reading the Gospel to him, Raskolnikov the murderer was, by no less astounding a miracle, transformed through the power of Christ into a follower and disciple: "I myself [was] a dead Lazarus, but Christ resurrected me."*

you have defiled!" Precisely because Sonia knew that the story was true, it was through the history of Jesus' miracle of the raising of Lazarus that Raskolnikov came to an authentic awareness of himself and to a sense of kinship with the earth. The full poetic meaning of this reconciliation and identification with Christ becomes evident from an unused entry in Dostoevsky's notebook for the novel:

> Now, kiss the Bible, kiss it, now read.
> [Lazarus come forth.]
> [And later when Svidrigaylov gives her money]
> "I myself [was] a dead Lazarus, but Christ resurrected me."
> N.B. Sonia follows him to Golgotha, forty steps behind.

And that Christ, too, was the Poet of the Spirit.

In the beauty of the lilies Christ was born across the sea,
With a glory in His bosom that transfigures you and me,
As He died to make men holy, let us die to make men free,
While God is marching on.
—*Julia Ward Howe,* The Battle Hymn of the Republic

17 ✛ The Liberator

The same nineteenth-century Russian writer whose narrative of Sonia and Raskolnikov gave such vivid expression to the perception of Jesus as Poet of the Spirit also articulated the meaning of Jesus the Liberator, in Ivan Karamazov's vision of the Grand Inquisitor. Christ returned to earth, but once again he was arrested, by orders of the Grand Inquisitor, and was confronted by this spokesman for an institutional Christianity that had finally corrected all the mistakes Jesus made while he was on earth. But Jesus the Prisoner was in fact Jesus the Liberator, as the Inquisitor acknowledged when he rehearsed the questions that Satan had addressed to Jesus during the temptation in the wilderness. The first of these, "If you are the Son of God, command these stones to become loaves of bread" (Matt. 4:3), presented the choice between

"You will know the truth, and the truth will make you free," Jesus the Liberator had promised (John 8:32). But according to the Grand Inquisitor in Dostoyevsky's Brothers Karamazov, *that promise was dangerous; and ever since then people had been coming to the powers of church and state to "lay their freedom at our feet, and say to us, 'Make us your slaves, but feed us.'" Therefore Christ's return to the streets of Seville was a threat, and the Inquisitor ordered him to "go, and come no more." And the legend concludes: "The Prisoner went away."*

turning the stones into bread so that "mankind will run after thee like a flock of sheep, grateful and obedient," and "some promise of freedom which men in their simplicity and their natural unruliness cannot even understand"; "for nothing has ever been more insupportable for a man and a human society than freedom." Jesus chose to be the Liberator rather than the Bread King, but in that he was mistaken. The freedom he offered was only for the elite. Ever since that mistake, his followers had been coming to the powers of the earth in both church and state, to "lay their freedom at our feet, and say to us, 'Make us your slaves, but feed us.'" When the Inquisitor had finished his commentary on the temptation of Jesus, "he waited some time for his Prisoner to answer him. . . . But [Jesus] suddenly approached the old man in silence, and softly kissed him on his bloodless aged lips. That was all his answer. The old man shuddered. His lips moved. He went to the door, opened it, and said to him: 'Go, and come no more. . . . come not at all, never, never!' And he let Him out into the dark alleys of the town. The Prisoner went away."

Alongside the conventional portraits of Jesus as the pillar of the status quo in state and church there had been a continuing tradition of describing him as the Liberator. But it was above all in the nineteenth and twentieth centuries that he became Jesus the Liberator, who overthrew empires, even so-called Christian empires. The agenda of liberation in Jesus Christ was formulated in the Magna Charta of Christian liberty: "There is neither Jew nor Greek, there is neither slave nor free, there is neither male nor female; for you are all one in Christ Jesus" (Gal. 3:28). Each of these three captivities has been justified in the name of Christ the Lord but has finally been challenged and overcome in the name of Jesus the Liberator.

The most persistent test case for the relevance of Jesus the Liberator to the social order was slavery. Both sides in that debate appealed to the authority of the person of Jesus. Both sides, Abraham Lincoln said, "read the same Bible, and pray to the same God; and each invokes his aid against the other." As he pointed out, "It may seem strange that any men should dare to ask a just God's assistance in wringing their bread from the sweat of other men's faces." But he added, quoting the commandment of Jesus, "Let us judge not, that we be not judged" (Matt. 7:1). Above all because of Lincoln's awareness that "since man is finite he can never be absolutely sure that he rightly senses the will of the infinite God," he is "in a real sense the spiritual center of American history." To an abolitionist like James Russell Lowell, the authority of Jesus for the situation was less equivocal:

> Once to every man and nation
> Comes the moment to decide,
> In the strife of truth with falsehood,
> For the good or evil side;
> Some great cause, God's new Messiah,
> Offering each the bloom or blight,
> And the choice goes by for ever
> 'Twixt that darkness and that light.
>
> By the light of burning martyrs
> Jesus' bleeding feet I track,
> Toiling up new Calvaries ever
> With the cross that turns not back;
> New occasions teach new duties,
> Time makes ancient good uncouth;
> They must upward still, and onward,
> Who would keep abreast of truth.

Steeped in the language and imagery of the English Bible but never really at home in any of the churches, Abraham Lincoln cherished a sense of reverence for the person of Christ in combination with a sense of ambiguity about any simple application of his teachings to society. A combination of his political sensitivity and his moral sense finally overcame the ambiguity: a political cartoon of 1862 shows him as the Great Emancipator shortly before his Emancipation Proclamation of 1 January 1863. He was assassinated on 14 April 1865.

The tension over what Jesus the Liberator meant for the institution of slavery seems to have been present in the Gospel portraits of Jesus themselves. Augustine declared it to have been the original intention of the Creator "that his rational creature should not have dominion over anything but the irrational creation—not man over man, but man over the beasts." Yet in a fallen world, slavery, like other imperfect institutions, had to be tolerated, and the authority of Christ the Liberator could not justify overthrowing it by force. The most compelling testimony for such social conservatism was found in the epistle of Paul to Philemon, in which Paul informed Philemon, a slaveholder, that he was sending Onesimus, a runaway slave, back to him, in order "to do nothing without your consent." He declined to compel Philemon to set Onesimus free as a matter of Christian duty, and he did not address the general question of the Christian attitude toward slavery as an institution. Those who continued to find that institution tolerable could thus lay claim to the letter of the New Testament. By their reading, it was no more legitimate to employ the sayings of Jesus as a weapon against slavery than it was to use his language about the kingdom of God to denounce all earthly kingdoms as usurpations. But the spirit of the epistle to Philemon, if not the letter, did call the institution of slavery into question, and new occasions did teach new duties, although it was a long time indeed before the recognition of those new duties produced decisive action.

EMANCIPATION OF THE SLAVES.
Proclamed on the 22d September 1862 by ABRAHAM LINCOLN, President of the United States of North America.

Combining elements from his Hindu tradition with his radical reading of the teachings of Jesus the Liberator in the Gospels, as he had learned this from Tolstoy's The Kingdom of God Is Within You, *Mohandas K. Gandhi developed nonresistance into a religious philosophy and a political strategy. In its name he defied and defeated imperialism, even though on 30 January 1948 he himself was assassinated in the process.*

Not only in Abraham Lincoln's America but as far away as the Netherlands and Suriname (Dutch Guiana) in South America, 1863 was the banner year for the emancipation of the slaves. Bearing the words "Emancipation of the Slaves in Suriname 1 July 1863," a commemorative seventieth-anniversary plate by C. Jetses (opposite page, right) gave credit for this gift of freedom to Christ the Liberator, worshiped by both slaves and slaveholders.

The Reverend Dr. Martin Luther King, Jr., was the most articulate spokesman of the civil rights movement, leader of its marches, strategist of its campaigns. Still it must never be forgotten that this minister of Jesus Christ saw all of this as the path of following Jesus in radical obedience and discipleship, which, as he said, drew him back "to the Sermon on the Mount, with its sublime teachings on love, and to the Gandhian method of nonviolent resistance." And it would cost him his life.

The rediscovery of Jesus the Liberator was confined neither to the debate over slavery nor to British and American thought. Perhaps the most widely celebrated such rediscovery in the nineteenth century was that of Leo Tolstoy. In *Resurrection,* the contrast between the Liberator and an inquisitor appears, once again in a prison, where a visitor "was startled to see a large picture of the Crucifixion, hanging in an alcove. 'What's that here for?' he wondered, his mind involuntarily connecting the image of Christ with liberation and not with captivity." Tolstoy's message was that the teachings of Jesus were to be taken literally. The final chapter of the novel is a commentary on the Sermon on the Mount, in which the protagonist "pictured to himself what this life might be like if people were taught to obey these commandments." Ecstasy came over him; "it was as though, after long pining and suffering, he had suddenly found peace and liberation."

Tolstoy's radical Christianity drew the excommunication of the Russian Orthodox church, but his reinterpretation of the message of Jesus also drew the devoted attention of many thousands. In his philosophy, as Isaiah Berlin has put it, Tolstoy "believed only in one vast, unitary whole," which he finally formulated as "a simple Christian ethic divorced from any complex theology or metaphysic . . . , the necessity of expelling everything that does not submit to some very general, very simple standard: say, what peasants like or dislike, or what the gospels declare to be good," two standards that were often the same. To most prophets of liberation and champions of the oppressed, Tolstoy's literal application

of the words of Jesus about nonviolence seemed the height of impracticality, a capitulation to injustice, indeed "the opium of the masses."

One exception was a young Indian-born barrister in South Africa. Tolstoy's book *The Kingdom of God Is within You,* he was to write later, "overwhelmed me. . . . Before the independent thinking, profound morality, and the truthfulness of this book, all [other Christian] . . . books . . . seemed to pale into insignificance." To this admirer Tolstoy wrote a letter (in English) on 7 September 1910 that became his religious-philosophical last will and testament: "The longer I live, and especially now when I feel keenly the nearness of death, I want to tell others what I feel so particularly keenly about, and what in my opinion is of enormous importance, namely what is called non-resistance, but what is essentially nothing other than the teaching of love undistorted by false interpretations. . . . This law has been proclaimed by all the world's sages, Indian, Chinese, Jewish, Greek and Roman. I think it has been expressed most clearly of all by Christ. . . . The whole of Christian civilisation, so brilliant on the surface, grew up on [an] obvious, strange, sometimes conscious but for the most part unconscious misunderstanding and contradiction [of the authentic teachings of Jesus the Liberator]." But soon "your British, as well as our Russian" government, with their nominal allegiance to the lordship of Jesus Christ, would have to face this contradiction and its consequences.

The name of Tolstoy's disciple was Mohandas K. Gandhi. His philosophy of "militant non-violence" was a blending of elements from traditional Hinduism and elements from Christianity or, more specifically, from the teachings of Jesus. Tolstoy's interpretations helped Gandhi to understand the authentic message of Jesus, and by the time Gandhi died a martyr on 30 January 1948, history had fulfilled Tolstoy's dying prophecy. "Your British" and "our Russian" empires, both of which had claimed to embody Christian values, had been overthrown. Yet Gandhi continued to have many disciples for his gospel of nonviolence in the spirit of Jesus the Liberator. There would be some whose path of following Jesus the Liberator took them the full distance from Palm Sunday to Good Friday, as the way of triumph became the way of the cross and the imitation of Christ took the form of being quite literally "made conformable unto his death" (Phil. 3:10). One of these was Martin Luther King, Jr., who was also martyred by an assassin's bullet, twenty years after Gandhi, on 4 April 1968.

Radical conformity to the life of Jesus, even to his death, and revolutionary obedience to his imperatives were not alien to the traditions out of which Martin Luther King, Jr., came. Both as an African American and as an American Baptist in the spiritual lineage of the Anabaptists, he was descended from forebears who had often been obliged to learn the cost of discipleship by suffering oppression and even death. The death of Mohandas K. Gandhi coincided with King's seminary matriculation. Gandhi had expressed the hope that it would be through American blacks "that the unadulterated message of nonvio-

lence will be delivered to the world." It was Mordecai Johnson, a leading black thinker, who brought the young theological student face to face with the thought of Gandhi as an eminently workable contemporary system. Johnson aroused in him the conviction that Gandhi was "the first person in history to live the love ethic of Jesus above mere interaction between individuals." Years later, in his last book, he was still citing Gandhi against the "nihilistic philosophy" and hatred that threatened to make his revolution "bloody and violent." "What was new about Mahatma Gandhi's movement in India," King declared, "was that he mounted a revolution on hope and love, hope and nonviolence."

That interpretation of the teaching of Jesus represented the intellectual and moral foundation of King's thought and action. As he would later reminisce, "When the protest began, my mind, consciously or unconsciously, was driven back to the Sermon on the Mount, with its sublime teachings on love, and to the Gandhian method of nonviolent resistance." Its accents ring out in such public documents as his "Letter from Birmingham Jail," in which he voiced the prophetic hope that "one day the South will know that when these disinherited children of God sat down at lunch counters, they were in fact standing up for what is best in the American dream and for the most sacred values in our Judeo-Christian heritage." This sounded naive to all of his critics and even to some of his supporters, as well as to those scholarly interpreters of the Gospels who had concluded that the message of Jesus was a "consistent eschatology" not intended for this world. But King's interpretation of the Sermon on the Mount was in fact a carefully thought-out and highly sophisticated strategy. In his series of nonviolent campaigns, King put that strategy to the test. Even many of his followers, both black and white, urged that the time for nonviolence had passed. Repeatedly he acknowledged that he was finding their impatient arguments increasingly persuasive, their strategies of direct action more tempting. Yet each time he ended up reaffirming his fundamental commitment to the practicality of the teachings of the Sermon on the Mount as a political program for the liberation of African Americans. At the heart of this program was the vision of human society as a "beloved community" of love and justice, to which, through power, even the recalcitrant would have to conform.

When I once asked my late colleague Charles Davis why Martin Luther King, Jr., had not become a Marxist and why those who followed him had accepted his philosophy of nonviolence, he unhesitatingly replied: "Because of the overpowering force of the figure of Jesus." That was also the reason in many cases for the positive response, painfully slow in coming though it was, that King's message called forth in white Christians. Obviously there remained a large group who did not respond positively, and Martin Luther King, Jr., became their victim, as he had long known he might. But in his death he carried out what he knew in his life, that he had been called to follow in the footsteps of Another. When he accepted the Nobel Peace Prize in December 1963, he repeated the commands and the promises of Jesus in the gospel of liberation as enunciated in the Sermon on the Mount:

"Peculiar institution" or not, the slavery and oppression from which Christ liberates humanity cannot be called a gentle thing. Consequently, to oppressor and oppressed alike, the liberation that his cross grants by whatever means may likewise appear extremely dramatic and even grotesque: "as one from whom men hide their faces he was despised" (Isa. 53:3).

"When the years have rolled past and when the blazing light of truth is focused on this marvelous age in which we live, men and women will know and children will be taught that we have a finer land, a better people, a more noble civilization, because these humble children of God were willing to 'suffer for righteousness' sake' (Matt. 5:10)."

In spite of its ambiguity, theological no less than political, such a reading of the message of Jesus continues to inspire the campaign for human liberation, in which Jesus the Liberator is being pitted against all the Grand Inquisitors, whether sacred or secular. But now he is often seen as inverting his original statement (Matt. 4:4) to read that man shall not live by the word of God alone but by bread as well, as sanctioning not only militant nonviolence but direct action, as not only blessing a spiritual poverty that awaits supernatural goods in the life to come but leading the poor of this world to natural goods in this life and in this world. The contrast between this picture of Jesus the Liberator and earlier pictures of Jesus the Liberator may perhaps be illumined by a comparison between the two versions of one of the Beatitudes. As the advocates of a nonpolitical interpretation of Christ the Liberator have always pointed out, the more familiar version in the Gospel of Matthew reads, "Blessed are the poor *in spirit,* for theirs is the kingdom of heaven" (Matt. 5:3). Yet the theology of liberation is based on the reminder that in the Gospel of Luke, Jesus cries out, "Blessed are you poor . . . , but woe to you that are rich!" (Luke 6:20, 24). If Dostoyevsky's legend of the Grand Inquisitor was the most profound portrayal of Jesus the Liberator, it was the American War between the States that evoked not only Lincoln's recognition of the ambiguity in citing Jesus as an authority for specific political action but also the most stirring summons ever penned to live and die in the name of Jesus the political Liberator, Julia Ward Howe's "Battle Hymn of the Republic," which supplies the epigraph for this chapter.

The teachings of Jesus did not condemn slavery, but slavery contradicted the spirit of Jesus the Liberator. That contradiction came to voice in the writings of two women. As the daughter of one theologian, Lyman Beecher, and the wife of another, Calvin Ellis Stowe, Harriet Beecher Stowe (lower right) agonized over the contradiction, and in Uncle Tom's Cabin *of 1852 produced a tract for the times, summoning a supposedly Christian America to throw off the yoke of slavery. Julia Ward Howe, shown here in her later years, articulated the summons in a poem that became the unofficial national anthem, whose final and climactic stanza was a cry of freedom in the name of Christ: "As He died to make men holy, let us die to make men free, / While God is marching on."*

Jesus shall reign where'er the sun
Does his successive journeys run,
His kingdom stretch from shore to shore
Till moons shall wax and wane no more.
People and realms of every tongue
Dwell on his love with sweetest song.
—*Isaac Watts,* Psalms of David

18 ❖ The Man Who Belongs to the World

Nazareth was what is known in colloquial English as a hick town, an insignif-
icant village, and Jesus of Nazareth was a provincial. When he described how
"the rulers of the Gentiles lord it over them, and their great men exercise authority over them" (Matt. 20:25), he was describing a phenomenon that belonged to a world far removed from his own. And even when, in an appearance
after the resurrection, he is represented by the author of the Acts of the Apostles as having referred to all of the outside world, it was as a provincial might,
dividing the world into the immediate environs and everything that was elsewhere (Acts 1:8): "Ye shall be witnesses unto me both in Jerusalem, and in all
Judea, and in Samaria—and unto the uttermost part of the earth." Therefore
his cosmopolitan detractors in the Roman empire were able to sneer that he

Jesus became the Man who Belongs to the World when the missionary journeys of his first apostles took them beyond Palestine, and then beyond Asia Minor, to the continent of Europe and to Rome. Twentieth-century European artists such as Georges Rouault have continued to search for a new idiom in which to express that universality, which has now encircled the globe.

had put in his appearance "in some small corner of the earth somewhere."

Jesus of Nazareth may have been a provincial, but Jesus Christ is the Man Who Belongs to the World, on whose empire the sun never sets. His name has come to be known "unto the uttermost part of the earth." In 1719, when the English hymn writer Isaac Watts published the poem that forms the epigraph to this chapter, the most dramatic growth in the extension of his influence ever known was just beginning. Because of that quantum increase, the best-known history of Christian expansion in English, that of Kenneth Scott Latourette, devoted three of its seven volumes to the nineteenth century alone, calling it *The Great Century*. Not coincidentally, the great century of Christian missionary expansion was also the great century of European colonialism. In consequence, although Jesus himself had lived in the Near East, it was as a religion of Europe that his message came— in the sense both of a religion *from* Europe and, often, a religion *about* Europe. Indeed, on the eve of the First World War, the provocative aphorism was coined, apparently by Hilaire Belloc: "The faith is Europe, and Europe is the faith." This seemed to imply that those who adopted European civilization came under pressure to undergo conversion to the European faith in Jesus Christ and that faith in Jesus Christ must be on European terms.

It is an oversimplification to dismiss the missions as nothing more than a cloak for white imperialism. Such an oversimplification ignores the biographical, religious, and political realities that run through the history of Christian missions during the great century and long before, as missionaries have, in the name of Jesus, striven to understand and learned to respect the particularity of the cultures to which they have come. The most celebrated instance of this was the work of the Jesuit Matteo Ricci in China. The first generation of Jesuits, under the leadership and inspiration of Francis Xavier, had followed the medieval pattern of the Western church, introducing the Roman Catholic liturgy of the Mass, forbidding any of the vernaculars in worship, and enforcing the use of Latin. With Ricci's arrival at Macau in 1582, that strategy underwent drastic revision. He adopted the monastic habit of a Buddhist monk, then the garb of a Confucian scholar, and became a renowned authority both in the natural sciences and in the history and literature of China. This erudition enabled him to present the person and message of Jesus as the fulfillment of the historic aspirations of Chinese culture. The Chinese, Ricci maintained, "could certainly become Christians, since the essence of their doctrine contains nothing contrary to the essence of the Catholic faith, nor would the Catholic faith hinder them in any way, but would indeed aid in that attainment of the quiet and peace of the republic which their books claim as their goal." Ricci remained an orthodox Catholic believer, whose very orthodoxy impelled him to take seriously the integrity of Chinese traditions. Similarly, although less dramatically, Roman Catholic and Protestant missionaries in the nineteenth century often managed to combine a commitment to evangelization in the name of Jesus with a deep (and ever deepening) respect for indigenous traditions.

In Monika Liu Ho-Peh's Stilling of the Tempest, *a Chinese Jesus, standing in the prow of the boat, rebukes the waves and commands, "Peace! Be still!" (Mark 4:39), as his terrified Chinese disciples—most of them bearded, as in Western art, but with Oriental features—strain at the oars and tug at the flapping sails.*

The blending of cultural traditions to make the universality of Jesus visible could take bizarre forms, as when an artist in India located the ascension of Christ in what is evidently an Indian scene, portrayed his followers as belonging to various nations—and clothed the ascending figure of the Savior in the garb of a Jesuit priest.

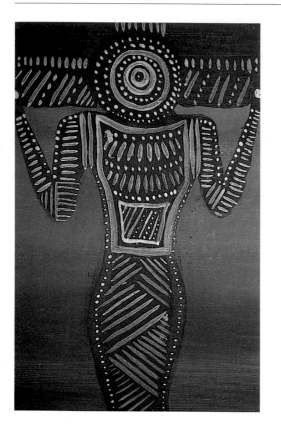

As seen by an Australian aboriginal, Miriam Rose Ungunmerr-Baumann, the crucifixion of Christ, which is part of the fourteen stations of the cross, has infinite score lines on the cross and on his arms to show the number of people for whom he was dying, as on the cross "his thoughts still move out in every direction to the people of the world."

As in the past, Christian missions in the nineteenth and twentieth centuries have involved many social changes. Perhaps the most important of these for the cultural development of the nations was the close association between the missions and the campaign for literacy. A monument to that achievement for the history of the Slavs is the very alphabet in which most Slavs write, called Cyrillic in honor of Saint Cyril. Not only among the Slavs in the ninth century, however, but also among the other so-called heathen in the nineteenth century, the two fundamental elements of missionary culture have been the translation of the Bible and education in the missionary schools. In one nation after another it was necessary, for the sake of translating the word of God, to reduce the language to written form, so that in many cases the first efforts ever at a scientific understanding of the language, by native or foreigner, came from Christian missionaries. They compiled the first dictionaries, wrote the first grammars, developed the first alphabets. Thus it came about that the first important proper name to have been written in many of these languages must have been the name of Jesus, with its pronunciation adapted to their distinctive phonic structure, just as it had been in all the languages of Europe. The Protestant missionary Bible societies have put at least the Gospels into an estimated two thousand languages or more.

Schools founded by Protestant missionary societies and Roman Catholic religious orders have been closely associated with this enterprise and have often functioned as the

The totem poles of the Pacific Northwest sometimes remind visitors of the Ruthwell Cross and other roadside crosses in Europe. Combining the two, Stanley Peters locates a totemic Jesus on a cross to communicate the mystery of Christ as truly the Man Who Belongs to the World.

centers for both the translation of the Gospels and the linguistic study undergirding it. This made them ambivalent about native culture, which the missionary teachers wanted to master in the name of Christ and felt obliged to exorcise also in the name of Christ because it was permeated with the spirit and superstition of heathenism. The memoirs of Asian and African graduates often express bitterness about the loss of native roots that was a by-product of such an education. Indian prime minister Jawaharlal Nehru, for example, was educated at Harrow and Cambridge, becoming, in his own eloquent phrase, "a

During the twentieth century even the traditional Christian cultures of the West reached out for innovative ways of portraying Jesus Christ as the Man Who Belongs to the World. In The Crèche by the Italian-American painter Joseph Stella, the Shepherds of Bethlehem and the Wise Men from the East stand for "all tribes and peoples and tongues" (Rev. 7:9) as well as for all social and economic classes, united in the worship of the Child.

Simultaneously traditional and innovative, Mount Calvary *by William Johnson (opposite page) comes out of the Christian tradition of the American black community and makes the four biblical figures, including Jesus (whose skin was probably quite dark) just as black as they had been Italian in the works of Florentine artists and Germanic in the works of Flemish artists.*

The process of "acculturation," by which the faith in Jesus Christ as not only the European Savior but the Man Who Belongs to the World finds equally legitimate expressions in symbols and art forms that come from non-European cultures, allows this traditional Igbo white-faced mask from eastern Nigeria to bear on its crest a depiction of Christ flanked by two angels.

queer mixture of the East and West, out of place everywhere, at home nowhere" and sensing a profound alienation between himself and the religion of the common people of India—as well as between himself and the Christianity of the British missionaries. Thus it was with a grim literalness that there was fulfilled, in the life of entire cultures, the saying of Jesus in the Gospels: "I have come to set a man against his father, and a daughter against her mother, and a daughter-in-law against her mother-in-law; and a man's foes will be those of his own household" (Matt. 10:35–36).

Yet the churches, too, early recognized, sometimes far more explicitly in the mission field than at home, that it was not enough to bring words about Jesus to the non-Christian world. It had not been enough in the days of Jesus, either, and so he had come as a healer and not only as a teacher. Similarly, in the second and third centuries Christianity "deliberately and consciously . . . assumed the form of 'the religion of salvation or healing,' or 'the medicine of soul and body,' and at the same time it recognized that one of its chief duties was to care assiduously for the sick in body." This succinct description by Adolf von Harnack could apply as easily to the nineteenth and twentieth centuries as to the second and third. The closing chapter of the New Testament depicted the city of God, with the throne of Jesus Christ the Lamb of God and the tree of life, and explained that "the leaves of the tree were for the healing of the nations" (Rev. 22:2).

In an age in which the healing of the nations from the ravages of hunger, disease, and war has become the dominant moral imperative, Jesus the Healer has assumed a central place. Yet the connection between evangelization in the name of Jesus and the mission of help and healing has also been an issue for debate, which comes as a commentary on the literal meaning of a word in the Gospels: "Whosoever shall give you a cup of water to drink in my name, because ye belong to Christ, verily I say unto you, he shall not lose his reward" (Mark 9:41). Some have named the name of Christ, clarifying its doctrinal and theological meaning, but without giving the cup of water; others have given the cup of water, providing the healing and improving the social lot of the disadvantaged, but without explicitly naming the name of Christ and the doctrine about his person. Is each of these only a partial obedience to this dual summons of Jesus?

A growing feature of the debate has been the stress on cooperation rather than competition between the disciples of Jesus and those who follow other ancient Teachers of the Way. Followers of Jesus who advocate such cooperation insist that they are no less committed to the universality of his person and message than are the advocates of the traditional methods of conquest through evangelization. The universality of Jesus, they urge, does not establish itself in the world through the obliteration of whatever elements of light and truth have already been granted to the nations of the world. For whatever the proximate and historical sources of that truth may have been, its ultimate source is God, the same God whom Jesus called Father; else the confession of the oneness of God is empty. Jesus was the Man Who Belongs to the World because he made it possible to appreciate more profoundly the full scope of the revelation of God wherever it had appeared in the history of the world, in the light of which his own meaning and message acquired more profound significance. In the eloquent paradox articulated by Archbishop Nathan Söderblom in his Gifford Lectures of 1931, "the uniqueness of Christ as the historical revealer, as the Word made flesh, and the mystery of Calvary," which are an "essentially unique character of Christianity," compel the affirmation that "God reveals himself in history, outside the Church as well as in it." So drastic a revision of the traditional Christian understanding that "there is salvation in no one else [than Jesus], for there is no other name under heaven given among men by which we must be saved" (Acts 4:12), would inevitably evoke vigorous discussion.

Such proposals for redefining the universality of Jesus came just as scholars in the West were giving new attention to the languages and cultures of other religious traditions. In 1875, Friedrich Max Müller began the publication of the monumental *Sacred Books of the East* in fifty-one volumes, opening the riches of the Eastern religious sages to readers who could not study the originals. In 1893, a World Parliament of Religions was held to draw the religious implications of the stubborn fact that the human race was not exclusively European and therefore not exclusively Christian. As the percentage of Christians in the total world population continues to decline, it seems inconceivable that the Christian church will ever replace all the other religions of humanity. If Jesus is to be the Man Who Belongs to the World, it will have to be by some other way.

The most remarkable document to come out of this deepening sense of a new universalism was published on 28 October 1965: the Declaration on the Relationship of the Church to Non-Christian Religions, *Nostra aetate,* of the Second Vatican Council. After a succinct and fair description of the religious quest and spiritual values at work in primitive religion, in Hinduism, in Buddhism, and in Islam, the council declared in a historic affirmation: "The Catholic Church rejects nothing which is true and holy in those religions. She looks with sincere respect upon those ways of conduct and of life, those rules and teachings which, though differing in many particulars from what she holds and sets forth, nevertheless often reflect a ray of that Truth which enlightens all men (John 1:9). Indeed, she proclaims and must ever proclaim Christ, 'the way, the truth, and the life' (John 14:6), in whom men find the fullness of religious life, and in whom God has reconciled all things to Himself." These two passages from the Gospel of John quoted in the decree clearly identify the issue. By citing the authority of both passages, the council sought to affirm universality and particularity simultaneously and to ground both of them in the figure of Jesus.

A special issue at the Second Vatican Council and throughout Christianity, particularly since the Second World War, was the relation between Christianity and the Jewish people, the people of Jesus; it was an issue that could not simply be subsumed under the general category of the world religions. The Holocaust took place in what had been nominally Christian territory, and among both Roman Catholics and Protestants in Germany there were those who, as the New Testament says about Paul's involvement in the martyrdom of Stephen, were "consenting to [the] death" of the Jews (Acts 8:1), and many more who were (as it seems now, by hindsight) blindly insensitive to the situation. The Second Vatican Council "deplores," it declared, "the hatred, persecutions, and displays of anti-Semitism directed against the Jews at any time and from any source," which would appear to include the official sources of the church's past. And it condemned any attempt to blame the death of Jesus "upon all the Jews then living, without distinction, or upon the Jews today," insisting that "the Jews should not be presented as repudiated or cursed by God."

This rethinking of the relation between Christianity and Judaism was partly the consequence of the worldwide horror over the Holocaust, but partly it also came through the most basic Christian reconsideration of the status of Judaism since the first century. Ironically, the years of Nazi anti-Semitism and the Holocaust in Germany had also been the years in which Christians developed that new awareness of the Jewishness of Jesus, the apostles, and the New Testament, which speaks in the language of the Vatican Council. For in 1933, the beginning of the Nazi era in Germany, there appeared, also in Germany, the first volume of one of the most influential biblical reference works of the twentieth century, the multivolume *Theological Dictionary of the New Testament,* which documented throughout that the teaching and language of the New Testament, including that of Jesus, cannot be understood apart from the context of Judaism. It was once again in the Gospel of John, despite the hostility of some of its language about Jews, that Jesus, speaking as a Jew to a non-Jew, was described as saying: "We [Jews] worship what we know, for salvation is from the Jews" (John 4:22). Directly he went on to say, in the next verse: "But the hour is coming, and now is, when the true worshipers [both Jews and Gentiles] will worship the Father in spirit and truth." Once again the theme is universality-with-particularity, as both of these are grounded in the figure of Jesus the Jew.

Like the familiar statue of
The Christ of the Andes *on the*
mountain border between Chile
and Argentina, this massive figure
in Rio de Janeiro represents Christ
offering a benediction and at the
same time extending an invitation,
not only to the people of Brazil but
to the whole human race to be
reconciled to God and to itself,
through the Man Who Belongs
to the World.

By a curious blend of these currents of religious faith and scholarship with the no less powerful influences of skepticism and religious relativism, the universality-with-particularity of Jesus has thus become an issue in the twentieth century not only for Christians but for humanity. The later chapters of this book show that as respect for the organized church has declined, reverence for Jesus has grown. For the unity and the variety of portraits of "Jesus through the centuries" have demonstrated that there is more in him than is dreamt of in the philosophy and christology of the theologians. Within the church, but also far beyond its walls, his person and message are, in the phrase of Augustine, a "beauty ever ancient, ever new," and now he belongs to the world.

ILLUSTRATION CREDITS

Illustrations are listed in order of appearance; page numbers are boldfaced.

Léon Augustin Lhermitte, *Friend of the Humble (Supper at Emmaus)* (detail), 1892. Courtesy of the Museum of Fine Arts, Boston. Gift of Randolph Coolidge **i**

Marco Palmezzano, *Christ Bearing the Cross* (detail), Pinacoteca, Vatican Museums (Scala/Art Resource, N.Y.) **ii**

The Savior, Russian icon, 16th c., Kremlin Armory, Kremlin, Moscow (Beniaminson/Art Resource, N.Y.) **vi**

Christ Pantocrator, 6th-c. encaustic icon, Holy Monastery of Saint Catherine at Sinai, Egypt **x** (detail), **1**

Samuel Lawrence, *Portrait of Alfred Lord Tennyson,* 1840, National Portrait Gallery, London **2**

Sir Francis Chantrey, *Arthur Henry Hallam,* pencil sketch, National Portrait Gallery, London **2**

The Ruthwell Cross, first half of the 8th c. (Photo: T. Middlemass, © Department of Archaeology, University of Durham, Durham, England) **3**

Masters of the Older Prayer Book of Maximilian I and Associates (Flemish, Ghent), *Hours of Queen Isabella the Catholic,* fol. 72v: *The Crucifixion,* and fol. 73r: *The Deposition,* c. 1497–1500. © Cleveland Museum of Art, Leonard C. Hanna, Jr., Fund, 1963.256 **4–5**

William Holman Hunt, *The Finding of the Saviour in the Temple* (detail), 1854–60, Birmingham Museums and Art Gallery, Birmingham, England **8**

Dieric Bouts, *Passover,* from *Altar of the Last Supper* (left wing), 1464–67, Collégiale Saint Pierre, Louvain, Belgium (Foto Marburg/Art Resource, N.Y.) **9**

Dante Gabriel Rossetti, *The Passover in the Holy Family* (detail), 1856, Tate Gallery, London (Tate Gallery/Art Resource, N.Y.) **10**

William Holman Hunt, *The Finding of the Saviour in the Temple,* 1854–60, Birmingham Museums and Art Gallery, Birmingham, England **11**

Enguerrand Quarton, *Pietà de Villeneuve d'Avignon,* 15th c., Musée du Louvre, Paris (Erich Lessing/Art Resource, N.Y.) **12**

James Jacques Joseph Tissot, *The Return of the Prodigal Son,* 1882, Collection Manney (Bridgeman/Art Resource, N.Y.) **13**

Eduard von Gebhardt, *The Sermon on the Mount,* Kloster Loccum, Germany (Photo: Heike Seewald) **14**

Lovis Corinth (after Rembrandt van Rijn), *The Sacrifice of Isaac,* 1920, Gift of the Marcy Family in Memory of Signert H. Marcy, © 1997 Board of Trustees, National Gallery of Art, Washington, D.C. **15**

Jerusalem (Photo: Stuart Franklin/Magnum Photos) **16**

From a late 17th-c. Qur'ān, Arabic MS 38, p. 35, Beinecke Rare Book and Manuscript Library, Yale University **17**

Tree of Jesse, 18th-c. icon from the Ionian Islands, part of a diptych. Richardson and Kailas Icons, London (Bridgeman/Art Resource, N.Y.) **18**

Marc Chagall, *Yellow Crucifixion,* 1943. © Centre Georges Pompidou, Paris (Photo: Phillipe Migéat) **20**

Matthias Grünewald, *Resurrection,* from the Isenheim Altarpiece, 1513–15, Musée Unterlinden, Colmar, France (Scala/Art Resource, N.Y.) **22** (detail), **23**

Albrecht Dürer, *Vision of the Seven Candlesticks,* woodcut, c. 1498, from the *Apocalypse* **25**

Luca Signorelli, *Trinity, Madonna, Archangels, and Saints Augustine and Athanasius,* c. 1514, Galleria Uffizi, Florence (Scala/Art Resource, N.Y.) **27**

Saint Augustine, beginning of *The City of God,* from the first edition, 1467, printed by Conrad Sweynheym and Arnold Pannartz at the Monastery of Subiaco **28**

Dieric Bouts, *Abraham and Melchizedek,* from *Altar of the Last Supper* (left wing), 1464–67, Collégiale Saint Pierre, Louvain, Belgium (Erich Lessing/Art Resource, N.Y.) **29**

Andreas Cellarius, "A Christianized Heaven, Southern Hemisphere," from *Atlas Coelestis seu Harmonia Macrocosmica,* 1660, Geography and Map Division, Library of Congress, Washington, D.C. **31**

Decorated initial page from Book I of Bede's *History of the English Church and People,* late 8th c. By permission of the British Library, Cotton Tiberius C II, fol. 5v **32**

Signaling Cuthbert's Death to Lindisfarne, illustration from Bede's prose *Life of Cuthbert,* late 12th c. By permission of the British Library, Yates Thompson MS 26, fol. 74v **33**

Circular map of the world, c. 1275. By permission of the British Library, Add. MS 28681 **34**

Fra Angelico, *Madonna and Christ Child Holding the Globe* (detail), 1433–35, Museo di San Marco, Florence (Nicolo Orsi Battaglini/Art Resource, N.Y.) **36**

Fra Angelico, *Madonna and Child with Eight Saints* (detail), 1438–52, Museo di San Marco, Florence (Scala/Art Resource, N.Y.) **37**

William Blake, *Dante at the Moment of Entering the Fire* (Purgatorio 27), 1824–27, National Gallery of Victoria, Felton Bequest, 1920 **39**

Michelangelo, *The Cumaean Sibyl,* 1510, Sistine Chapel, Vatican Palace (Scala/Art Resource, N.Y.) **40**

Michelangelo, *The Prophet Isaiah,* 1509–10, Sistine Chapel, Vatican Palace (Scala/Art Resource, N.Y.) **40**

"The Siren Painter," *The Ship of Ulysses and the Song of the Sirens* (detail from *stamnos* found at Vulci, 480–470 B.C. Copyright British Museum **41**

Lysippos, *Bust of Socrates* (copy of original), late 4th c. B.C., Musée du Louvre, Paris (Giraudon/Art Resource, N.Y.) **42**

Lady Philosophy, from Boethius's *De Consolatione Philosophiae,* MS 1253, fol. 2v/3r, Universitätsbibliothek, Leipzig **42**

Raphael, *Saint Paul Preaching at Athens,* 1515–16, Victoria and Albert Museum, Picture Library. By courtesy of the Board of Trustees of the Victoria and Albert Museum, London **44**

Hans Memling, *Christ as Salvator Mundi Amongst Musical Angels* (detail), c. 1487–90, Koninklijk Museum voor Schone Kunsten, Antwerp **46, 47**

Jacopo Tintoretto, *Christ Before Pilate,* 1566–67, Scuola di San Rocco, Venice (Scala/Art Resource, N.Y.) **48**

Giacomo Triga, *Meeting of Saint Ignatius the Martyr and Saint Polycarp at Smyrna,* San Clemente, Rome (Alinari/Art Resource, N.Y.) **49**

Constantine the Great Crowned by the Hand of God, medal, Kunsthistorisches Museum, Vienna **50**

Cesare Nebbia, *Council of Nicaea,* 16th-c. fresco, Biblioteca Apostolica, Vatican (Scala/Art Resource, N.Y.) **51**

Court of Emperor Justinian (detail of mosaic), San Vitale, Ravenna, Italy (Scala/Art Resource, N.Y.) **52**

Early view of Constantinople, from Cyril Mango, *Le développement urbain de Constantinople (IVe–VIIe siècles)* (Paris: Diffusion de Boccard, 1985) **53**

Raphael, *The Repulse of Attila,* c. 1513–14, Stanze di Raffaello, Vatican Palace (Scala/Art Resource, N.Y.) **54**

Charlemagne between two saints, from the burial shrine of Charlemagne, 1215, Cathedral Treasury, Palatine Chapel, Aachen, Germany (Scala/Art Resource, N.Y.) **55**

Christ Blessing, 13th-c. French enamel plaque, Musée Dobrée, Nantes, France (Giraudon/Art Resource, N.Y.) **56**

Byzantine mosaic of Christ, Hagia Sofia Museum, Istanbul, Turkey (Scala/Art Resource, N.Y.) **58**

Christ Pantocrator, apse mosaic, Duomo, Cefalu, Italy (Scala/Art Resource, N.Y.) **59**

Illustration from Dante's *Divine Comedy,* Primum Mobile, late 14th c., Cod. It. IX, 276 (=6902), fol. 73r, Biblioteca Nazionale Marciana, Venice **60**

Composite Icon with the Crucifixion, Christ in the Sepulcher, Saints, and Gospel Scenes, 11th–12th c., Hermitage Museum, Saint Petersburg **61**

Ashmole Bestiary, 1511, fol. 5, Bodleian Library, Oxford **62**

Pietro di Pucci da Orvieto, *Universe Supported by God with the Signs of the Planets,* Campo Santo, Pisa, Italy (Alinari/Art Resource, N.Y.) **63**

Canterbury Psalter, c. 1180–90, MS lat. 8846, fol. 1, Bibliothèque Nationale, Paris **64**

Theophan the Greek, *Transfiguration,* Tretyakov Gallery, Moscow (Scala/Art Resource, N.Y.) **68**

The Transfiguration of Christ, Russia, c. 1970, French crypt of the Patriarchal Orthodox Center, Geneva-Chambésy, Switzerland (Photo: Michel and Lieselotte Quenot) **69**

Antonella da Messina, *Christ at the Pillory,* 15th c., Musée du Louvre, Paris (Erich Lessing/Art Resource, N.Y.) **72**

Hans Memling, *The Passion of Christ* (detail), Galleria Saubauda, Turin, Italy (Scala/Art Resource, N.Y.) **73**

Master of the Bruges Passion Scenes, *Christ Presented to the People,* c. 1510, National Gallery, London. Reproduced by courtesy of the Trustees of the National Gallery **74**

Michelangelo, *The Creation of Adam,* 1511, Sistine Chapel, Vatican Palace (Scala/Art Resource, N.Y.) **76**

Michael Pacher, *Altarpiece of the Fathers of the Church* (detail), c. 1483, Alte Pinakothek, Munich (Art Resource, N.Y.) **77**

Sandro Botticelli, *Saint Augustine,* c. 1480, Chiesa di Ognissanti, Florence (Scala/Art Resource, N.Y.) **78**

Vittore Carpaccio, *Saint Augustine in His Study,* c. 1500, School of San Giorgio degli Schiavoni, Venice (Scala/Art Resource, N.Y.) **80**

Gerard David, *The Marriage at Cana,* c. 1500, Musée du Louvre, Paris (Scala/Art Resource, N.Y.) **82**

From a 15th-c. Indulgence scroll, MS 410 (England), Yale Collection of Early Books and Manuscript, Beinecke Rare Book and Manuscript Library, Yale University **172**

Lucas Cranach the Elder, woodcut for Luther's *Septembertestament* (Wittenberg, 1522) **173**

Lucas Cranach the Elder, *Portrait of the Young Martin Luther*, 1526, Germanisches Nationalmuseum, Nuremberg (Scala/Art Resource, N.Y.) **174**

J. S. Bach, *Saint Matthew Passion*, reprinted in *Johann Sebastian Bach: His Life, Times and Influence*, ed. Barbara Schwendowius and Wolfgang Dömling (New Haven and London: Yale University Press, 1984) **175**

B. Maura, *Fr. Luis de León*, engraving, 1884. Courtesy of Biblioteca Nacional, Madrid **176**

Hans Holbein the Younger, *Allegory of the Old and New Testaments*, c. 1530, National Gallery of Scotland **177**

Salvador Dali, *The Christ of Saint John of the Cross*, 1951, The Saint Mungo Museum of Religious Life and Art, Glasgow **178**

Lucas Cranach the Younger, *Die Erlösung*, 1555, Evangelische-Lutherische Kirchgemeinde, Weimar (Photo: Constantine Beyer) **179**

Promenade des Bastions, Geneva (Photo: Greg Christensen/Image Bank, N.Y.) **180**

F. Halpin, *Portrait of Roger Williams* (engraving), 1847. Courtesy of the Rhode Island Historical Society **181**

Mabuse (Jan Gossaert), *Christ, Mary, and Saint John the Baptist* (detail), Museo del Prado, Madrid **182**

The Rider on His White Horse (detail), from an early 14th-c. Apocalypse, Roy.19.B.XV, fol. 37. By permission of the British Library **183**

Sunday Morning on a Battleship at Sea (UPI/Corbis-Bettmann) **184**

The Rider on His White Horse, from an early 14th-c. Apocalypse, Roy.19.B.XV, fol. 37. By permission of the British Library **185**

"An Elizabethan Galleon," from *Iconography of Ships*. Courtesy of the Mariners' Museum, Newport News, Virginia **186**

Anna Hyatt Huntington, *Joan of Arc,* Munson-Williams-Proctor Institute Museum of Art, Utica, New York. Gift of the Scottish Deerhound Club of America **187**

William Otto Pitthan, *Thomas Münzerin in der Schlact bei Mühlhausen*, 1958, Deutscheshistorisches Museum, Berlin **188**

Warner Sallman, *The Christmas Story,* from *War Cry,* Christmas 1942. Courtesy of the Salvation Army **189**

Statue of Comenius, Moravian College (Photo: Stephen Barth/Moravian College) **190**

Edward Hicks, *The Peaceable Kingdom with Quakers Wearing Banners* (detail), 19th c., Yale University Art Gallery, Bequest of Robert W. Carle **191**

Somme American Cemetery near Bony, France (UPI/Corbis-Bettmann) **192**

Léon Augustin Lhermitte, *Friend of the Humble (Supper at Emmaus)* (detail), 1892. Courtesy of the Museum of Fine Arts, Boston. Gift of Randolph Coolidge **194**

Benjamin West, *Christ's Blessing* (detail), c. 1777. Courtesy of Saint Pancras Parochial Church, London **195**

Samuel Watson, astronomical clock (detail of dial), late 17th c., Windsor Castle, The Royal Collection, © Her Majesty Queen Elizabeth II **196**

Max Liebermann, *The Twelve-Year-Old Jesus in the Temple*, 1879, Hamburger Kunsthalle, Hamburg (Photo © Elke Walford, Hamburg) **197**

Caravaggio, *Supper at Emmaus*, 1601, National Gallery, London. Reproduced by courtesy of the Trustees of the National Gallery **198**

Charles-Alphonse Dufresnoy, *The Death of Socrates*, Galleria Palatina, Palazzo Pitti, Florence (Alinari/Art Resource, N.Y.) **200**

Thomas Sully, *Thomas Jefferson*, 1822, The West Point Museum, United States Military Academy, West Point, New York **201**

Thomas Jefferson, pages from Jefferson's *The Life and Morals of Jesus of Nazareth*, facsimile ed. (Washington, D.C.: Government Printing Office, 1904) **201**

Reuben Moulthrop, *Ezra Stiles*, 1794, Yale University Art Gallery. Gift of the Reverend Ezra Stiles Gannett, B.A. (Hon.) 1820 **202**

George Dunlop Leslie (after Mason Chamberlin), *Benjamin Franklin*, c. 1856, Yale University Art Gallery. Gift of Avery Rockefeller for the University Library **203**

Gustave Doré, *Christ Leaving the Praetorian* (detail), Musée des Beaux-Arts, Nantes, France (Giraudon/Art Resource, N.Y.) **206**

Gustave Doré, *Heaven of Mars: The Cross*, 1868 (Photo: Yale Audio-Visual Department) **207**

Ralph Waldo Emerson. Courtesy of the Harvard University Archives **208**

Gerrit van Honthorst, *Adoration of the Child,* Galleria Uffizi, Florence (Scala/Art Resource, N.Y.) **209**

Ivan Kramskoy, *Christ in the Desert*, 1872–74, Tretyakov Gallery, Moscow (Scala/Art Resource, N.Y.) **210**

William Dyce, *The Woman of Samaria*, c. 1860, Birmingham Museums and Art Gallery, Birmingham, England **211**

Fritz von Uhde, *Let the Children Come to Me*, 1884, Museum der Bildenden Künste, Leipzig **212**

Heinrich Hofmann, *Jesus in the Garden of Gethsemane*, 1890, reprinted with permission of the Riverside Church and New York Graphic Society, all rights reserved **214**

Caspar David Friedrich, *The Cross in the Mountains*, 1880, Gemäldegalerie, Staatliche Kunstammlungen, Dresden (Erich Lessing/Art Resource, N.Y.) **216**

William Blake, *The Resurrection*, 1805. Courtesy of the Fogg Art Museum, Harvard University Art Museums. Bequest of Grenville N. Winthrop **217**

Albert Pinkham Ryder, *Christ Appearing to Mary*, c. 1885, National Museum of American Art, Washington, D.C. (National Museum of American Art/Art Resource, N.Y.) **218**

Sir John Everett Millais, *Portrait of John Henry Newman.* Courtesy of the National Portrait Gallery, London **219**

Benjamin Kopman, "Sonia and Raskolnikov," from Fyodor Dostoevsky's *Crime and Punishment,* trans. Constance Garnett (New York, 1956) **220**

Piero della Francesca, *Resurrection* (detail), late 1450s, Pinacoteca Comunale, Sansepolcro (Scala/Art Resource, N.Y.) **222, 223**

William Sharp, "The Grand Inquisitor," from Fyodor Dostoyevsky's *The Brothers Karamazov,* trans. Constance Garnett (New York: Random House, 1943) **224**

"Abraham Lincoln: Emancipation of the Slaves," engraving, Library of Congress, Washington, D.C. **226**

C. Jetses, *Freedom as a Gift of Christ,* 1913. From Jan Pieterse, *White on Black* (New Haven and London: Yale University Press, 1992) **226**

Henri Cartier-Bresson, "Gandhi supported by his secretaries, making his pilgrimage to Nizm U Din, a Muslim Shrine," 1944 (Magnum Photos) **227**

"Dr. Martin Luther King tells Negros that they will not lose their fight for voter registration in Selma . . . February 22, 1965" (UPI/Corbis-Bettmann) **228**

José Clemente Orozco, *The Epic of American Civilization: Modern Migration of the Spirit* (Panel 21), 1932–34. Commissioned by the Trustees of Dartmouth College, Hanover, N.H. **230**

J. D. Wells, *Harriet Beecher Stowe,* c. 1852, Schlesinger Library, Radcliffe College, Cambridge, Mass. **232**

Julia Ward Howe, pictured in her later years (Corbis-Bettmann) **232**

Horace Pippin, *The Crucifixion*, 1943, Menil Collection, Houston, Texas **234**

François-Xavier Goddard, *Processional Cross: Figure of Christ as Mask*, Zaire, c. 1950 (Photo: Vivant Univers, Namur, Belgium) **235**

Georges Rouault, *The Holy Face,* Musée d'Art Moderne de la Ville de Paris (Giraudon/Art Resource, N.Y.) **237**

Monika Liu Ho-Peh, *The Stilling of the Tempest,* 1950s, from Arno Lehmann, *Christian Art in Africa and Asia* (Saint Louis, Mo.: Concordia, 1969) (Photo-Archiv des PGV, Aachen) **238**

The Ascension of Jesus Dressed as a Priest, Mughal, India. Edwin Binney III Collection, San Diego Museum of Art **239**

Miriam Rose Ungunmerr-Baumann, *Stations of the Cross: Twelfth Station, Crucifixion,* 1974–75, Daly River Mission Church, Northern Territory, Australia. Courtesy of the Bible Society of Australia **240**

Stanley Peters, *Totem Cross.* Reproduced by permission of the Canadian Conference of Catholic Bishops, Ottawa (Photo: Thomas E. Moore, copyright © 1976, all rights reserved) **241**

Joseph Stella, *The Crèche,* c. 1929–33. Collection of the Newark Museum, Newark, N.J. (Newark Museum/Art Resource, N.Y.) **242–43**

Igbo mask, 20th c., Nigeria, Collection of Ernst Anspach, New York (Werner Forman/Art Resource, N.Y.) **244**

William H. Johnson, *Mount Calvary,* c. 1944, National Museum of American Art, Washington, D.C. (National Museum of American Art/Art Resource, N.Y.) **245**

Statue of Christ, Rio de Janeiro (Photo: Bruno Barbey/Magnum Photos) **248**

INDEX